FROM STREET LIFE

AGAINST ALL ODDS

FROM STREET LIFE TO CHART LIFE

CONTENTS

PART 2
FIRST TASTE OF SUCCESS 72

PART 3
PUSHING ON AFTER BYRON 132

PART 4
N-DUBZ DOMINATION: TODAY AND TOMORROW 152

1

N-Dubz are
Britain's No. 1 band
according to the
Sun newspaper

3

number of MOBO
awards N-Dubz
have won

N-DUBZ IN

22

age in years of Dino
'Dappy' Contostavlos
and Richard
'Fazer' Rawson

500

number of pounds
spent on first video
'Every Day of My Life'

500,000

copies sold
of debut album
Uncle B

9,000,000

number of hits
'Ouch' has had
on YouTube

21

age in years
of Tulisa 'T'
Contostavlos

NUMBERS

45,000

number of pounds
spent on video for
'Playing with Fire'

10,000,000

number of
MySpace hits
N-Dubz had
in 2009

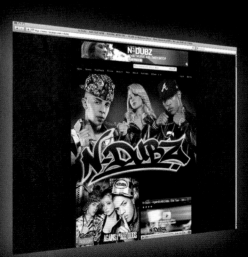

INTRO-DUCTION

NaNaNiiiii! Duku yourself for the support, people, a you dat! The Dynamic Trio and voice of the yoot dem N-Dubz inside de place.

Seriously, people, we could never have made it this far if it wasn't for you lot, so we knew it was time to pay you back with the only official N-Dubz book. **Boom!**

It's all in here. From what we were like at school as little rascals to what we're like on tour as the UK's most relevant band out there. We've raided the photo albums for pictures of us as kids and even included some shots from **you!** By the time you finish reading, you'll know exactly how we made a success of ourselves as well as everything that makes us tick.

People always ask us about our outlook on life, so let us try to break it down for you. The N-Dubz philosophy is look forward, be humble, know where you want to go in life and don't listen to anyone who tries to hold you back. If there's something you yearn for, don't let anyone tell you it's unreachable. Beat the system, live the dream, make money and get out of the hood, but also be passionate about what you do and enjoy yourself.

There are two main rules to live by, two tools that you can use: common sense and knowing right from wrong. If you use those two things, you'll go far. Just try and be as righteous as possible.

Believe you can achieve anything you want and if you work hard, it IS going to happen for you. There's only so much that can stop you. If you go to school, then uni, and study for what you want to do, there are only so many people that can turn you down before eventually you get your shot.

There are no excuses for not making something of yourself, it is all about hard work. If you have a goal, go for it. Always set your own path and never follow the trail even in the face of adversity.

Never doubt yourself, because if you do that, you limit yourself to what you can do. And who's going to believe in you if you don't even believe in yourself?

Duku yourself!

N-DUBZ OFFICIAL SLANGUAGE

Are u suuuuuuuick:	That's amazing
Duku yourself:	Big up yourself
D-A-P-'s to the Y:	Dappy
Seari 4 realli:	Are you being serious?
Bang bang shoes/whatever:	Nice shoes/whatever
FA Take It Easy:	Fazer
Maddas 4 ralles:	That's proper mad
NaNa:	Both hi and goodbye
Zoop zoop:	An expression of excitement about anything
Shabarky:	Someone's eyeing you up
A pinky:	A £50 note
N-Dublets:	N-Dubz fans
Weeeeeeeeeeeeeeee!:	In a high-pitched tone. Use it to embarrass someone if you catch them out
Say something:	What you gonna do about it? A way to end a conversation
Ha ha:	Official N-Dubz trademark
NaNaNiiiii:	Official N-Dubz trademark

9

PART 1
THE EARLY DAYS

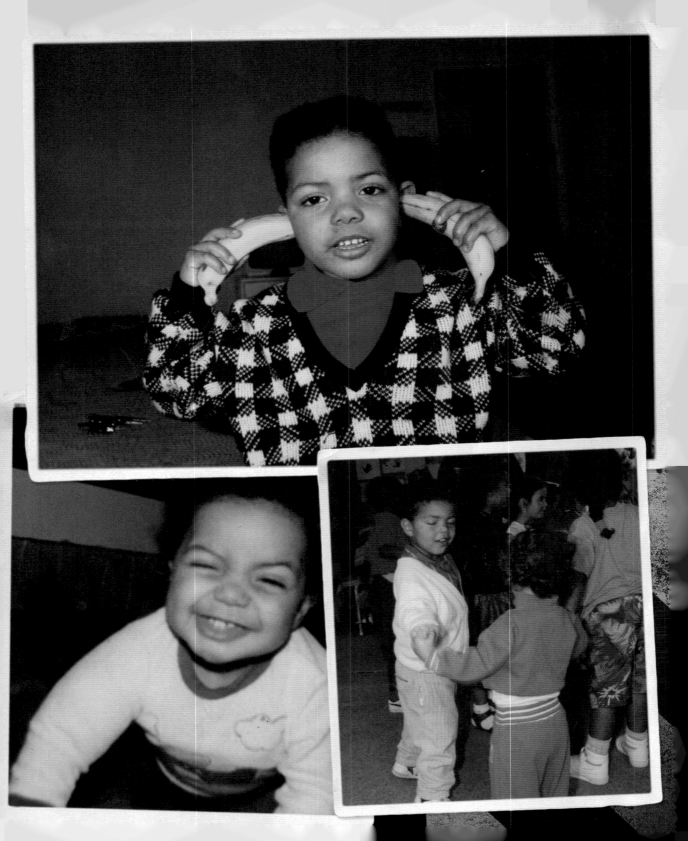

TEACHER'S PET... HATE!

If it wasn't for N-Dubz I'd most likely be dead or in prison, because school was never my thing. I went to Haverstock Secondary School in Camden and I ain't gonna candy-coat it and say I was an angel. I was pretty much kicked out of every lesson and teachers didn't really like me.

I don't think my music teacher liked me whatsoever. I was NEVER in his lesson – he'd kick me out every single time, even though I had a lot of talent for music. I was playing drums back then and I was playing piano too. I was only 12 at the time but it just didn't seem like he was interested.

My happiest memory as a youngster growing up was when I was doing athletics. I was really into sports and I got loads of gold medals between 12 and 16 when I was running for Camden and also running for London in the 1500 metres.

I got nuff gold medals and winners' ribbons at my house. I would have been in the Olympics if I hadn't started smoking and hanging around on the streets, I'm sure of it. I do have regrets about smoking, because now even just a run to the shops in the cold will kill my chest and that never would have happened to me back in the day.

I remember once I finished school and told my mate I'd race him back to our ends. He could take the bus and I would run it. It's about a mile and a half and I chased all the way up that road and beat him easily. I was waiting for him outside KFC and I wasn't even out of breath. If I tried to do that now I'm telling you I wouldn't even make it a quarter of the way up the road.

Apart from sports, I wasn't the best in school by a long way. I was always hanging around in groups of people, bunking off school with Dappy to go to his dad's recording studio.

My attendance record one year was something terrible like 28 per cent. And the few times when I was in, I wasn't even in the lessons because they'd kick me out. I wasn't properly bad, I just had a short attention span and I would be a bit disruptive. I'd get bored and start talking to people.

Most of the teachers just didn't want to know. I was always in headmaster's detention or in referral classes. They tried to expel me in my early teens, but my dad is proper democratic and good at talking.

I think racism was definitely part of the reason I didn't get along at school. Certain times the teachers would wind me up just to get me angry and get me out of the class. That's how I felt anyway. One teacher told me, 'You're just like all those black boys you read about in the newspapers blah blah blah ...' That's when my dad got involved and stood up to them so they couldn't expel me.

There was one teacher that understood me fully called Mr Crocker. He taught English and he was the best teacher I ever had in my school. He was my guy. Even when I'd get sent out

of other people's lessons I'd go over to his class and just chill. Anything he told me I would listen to him and take it seriously. I would stay in his lesson, and do all the work he wanted me to do, because he took the time to understand me as a person. He never judged me or tried to tell me I wouldn't achieve anything.

If all my teachers had been like Mr Crocker I reckon I would have come out with straight A grades. But because I didn't have any sort of support from the teachers I just thought 'nah' and messed around.

Teachers have a responsibility to make children believe they can achieve things. Teachers can't expect people to act like them if you come from different places. If my life ain't like yours, how am I gonna just behave like you do? You need to understand where I'm coming from and how I am as a person. A teacher should be able to understand that every child in the classroom is different, we don't just all conform to how they think things should be. That doesn't make us bad necessarily, just different.

There were a couple of teachers who were the exact opposite to Mr Crocker. There was one who always told me, 'One day I'm gonna come into McDonald's with my family and see you flipping burgers – if you're lucky enough to get a job there.'

Well, my little brother just finished at that school last year and I drove down there in my BMW X5 to pick him up and see all my old teachers. I saw that teacher and I was friendly. He came up to me and said, 'You're doing pretty well for yourself.'
I said, 'Yeah man, you're doing pretty shit for yourself – you're still here!' I saw his face go red and that was that.

Looking back on it, I wish I had been different at school. The thing is with me, anything I put my mind to, I become good at. I've got a very expandable and adaptable brain.

Luckily it's worked out for me, but if it hadn't, life would have been very different. I know I had talent, but I got lucky with it. You can't rely on that, so my advice to kids would be to stay in school.

That's what I said to my little brother. He's 18 soon and yeah, he's out on the streets, but he's not selling drugs or getting up to badness. I tell him, 'You go to college, bruv, and get your grades. Think about what you want to do and I will set you up in business.' I give him money for the weekend so he doesn't have to get into stuff and can concentrate on his studies.

My advice to other people would be get your grades. Be smart with what you're doing and get yourself into college. You need to have a certain amount of grades to get in there. There's no point in saying you're gonna go to college if you don't put the work in to get yourself there to start with. You won't get on the course.

If you want to set up your own plumbing company when you're older you need to do the foundation work starting at school age. You need to commit yourself to work early on.

There will always be setbacks and people trying to pull you down, but you have to focus and make it happen for you. If people try and diss you, just take that as creative criticism. If someone tells me I'm shit, I'll ask why. And if they can show me that something I said or did is shit, I will work on that so

no one can ever tell me that again. Keep an open mind and turn negatives into positives.

My mum knew I wanted to make music, get famous and be successful. I believed in myself the whole time.

> My parents were a good force in my life and one thing I would advise any parent is to encourage your child. If your child has a talent, then you need to push that. They believed in my talent and encouraged me. Even though when I was 16 my mum did start telling me to get a proper job! But she knew I wanted to make music, get famous and be successful. I believed in myself the whole time.

My mum would hear my tapes and tell me they were really good and give me the encouragement I needed to keep believing in myself. Kids need that in their lives.

MY SCHOOL HELL

I was a geek at school. As an only child, I went to school already quite a loner and even though I had some friends, I would always move around from group to group.

I'd always be the little odd one out. I was in a girls' school called La Sainte Union in Highgate until I was 12 and I wasn't very popular. I was quite pretty but that didn't get me anywhere. Some girls hated me because the older girls would call me pretty. I always wanted to be cool, but I never really was! I really wanted to fit in and be popular so I'd try and wear the right clothes and say the right things, but I always used to get it wrong when I was trying to impress people.

In the end I pretty much just gave up on having many friends there and was constantly by myself at playtime – not knowing what to do and lonely.

And I was a real scaredy-cat with the teachers, even though I was in all the top classes there. I was intelligent but quiet so I would never speak up or answer back. I always did whatever I was told and got my homework done on time.

I got really good grades – but having no friends was horrible and that's what made me want to move schools.

It all changed when I went to Dappy and Fazer's school, Haverstock, when I was 12. The day before I started, Dappy took me shopping to sort out my wardrobe. As my cousin he was the closest thing I had to a brother growing up, so he took it on himself to help me out. Plus he's a year older than me, so he was just that bit cooler in my eyes. My mum was still buying my clothes up until then.

He took me into JD Sports and Footlocker and bought me some Nike TNs and then a jumper from Gap and a baseball jacket with some Nike tracksuit bottoms. He even got one of his girl mates to come around and teach me how to slick my hair up and scrape it back. He sorted me out with some pre-training before I started there.

He also gave me a few tips about how to behave and who to avoid.

Because he was Mr Popular, that rubbed off on me as his cousin. And as it was a mixed-sex school the rules changed. If the guys liked you, then the girls wanted to be your friend too.

I remember how popular Dappy was when I was at Haverstock. One day I went in wearing a pair of his tracksuit bottoms he'd lent me. I left them in the changing room for PE and when I came back they'd been stolen. One of the girls had nicked them! Lol. I had to borrow a mate's tracksuit bottoms.

I really came out of my shell at Dappy's school and became a lot more sociable – even though I was still a geek at heart.

At Haverstock, drink and weed was a standard thing for everyone. The first time I got absolutely smashed was when I was 12 years old. I would drink the cheapest stuff available because I didn't have enough money as a young kid. So things like cider, vodka, beer – we'd convince older girls to buy it for us.

We'd be getting messy every weekend. I've never stopped drinking, but I stopped smoking weed when I was 14 as I started getting heart palpitations and having panic attacks. One day I fell to the floor, started frothing at the mouth and blacked out. I woke up in an ambulance and never smoked weed again. I've been left with heart palpitations and panic attacks to this day as a result of smoking – so let that be a warning to you! You never know how drugs will affect you – in my opinion, stay away.

The first few months of being at Haverstock were brilliant. I'd gone from being a loner to knowing everyone and being one of the most popular people in the school. I had so many friends – even though I soon found out most of them were fake – and everyone was just cool with me. I was chatting to guys and hanging out with the kids from the local estate who went to my school that I'd never met before. It was an amazing time for me. It was like a whole new world. I even went to under-18 raves and played out after school; I really came out of my shell.

But my education suffered. Haverstock was more like a play centre than a school. I was around kids that had no respect for their teachers whatsoever – none of them did any work and in class they spent the whole time

screaming at each other and cussing the teachers. I'd never seen anything like it before.

Because I wanted to be cool, I blended in with it and started not learning. I realised I didn't have to do work. No one else did and they were getting away with it.

It was a negative way of blending in, but for some reason part of being cool meant not listening to your teachers or doing your work. I don't think I did more than two days' worth of work in the whole year and a half that I was at Haverstock.

The good times didn't last longer than eight months though. Then the bullying started. First one girl decided to turn on me and made up a rumour. Someone told her I said something about her or some rubbish. I had never experienced aggression at that level before. She was screaming in my face with a pencil in her hand saying she was going to stab me with it.

From there it was like a trend. Another girl would come up to me and accuse me of saying something about her, and then another and another. I was only around 13 at this time but next came rumours about boys. I was a virgin at that age but still one girl would tell another girl that I'd had sex with her man – just to get me in trouble. So then loads of the girls in school started calling me a slag and a slut and making my life hell.

Sometimes a guy they fancied would ask me out instead of them and so they'd make up even more stuff about me to paint a bad picture of me.

All of the friends I thought I had made just turned out to be backstabbers or weak followers (sheep).

After about a year I eventually had enough and I started on a girl who I thought had been making up rumours about me. She wasn't a tough girl, but neither was I, and I didn't know that she was being bullied as well. So when I started arguing with her it was like the final straw and she flipped out and punched me in the face. I fought back but all my punches landed on her head so the wounds were hidden under her hair and you couldn't see that I'd really hit her. She split my lip and I was bleeding, so everyone said that she had won the fight.

From then on I was branded a pussy because I had been beaten up by a girl who wasn't even hard. That was it for me. They all started on me. Once they sensed weakness they were like vultures. In the end I got jumped by five girls who kicked the daylights out of me. I was on the floor covering my face, but they managed to get through so I ended up all bruised and with footprints on my face and head.

I had one proper friend left called Shereen who tried to stand up for me, and she said it was time to do something about it.

I wanted revenge. I was angry more than upset by now. I knew that if I didn't do something about that last beating, I could never show my face at that school again.

I started plotting what I could do with my friend. Then some of her friends got roped in and before I knew it the whole thing was starting to escalate into loads of people saying they were gonna get involved in some sort of massive street fight.

We spent a whole night training ourselves for what we were gonna do.

In the end, the news of what we were planning got back to my dad – and he hit the roof. He went mad at me, stamped it all out and that was the end of it. I'm glad he did, looking back on it, but it meant I couldn't go back to that school.

So from 14 I was out of school for almost a year. During that time I was just hanging out with my friends on the streets.

> **I started hanging out in a different area to stay away from those people, but every now and then I would have to go back to where they lived. I was seen as an easy target now and I'd have people ringing up my house saying they were gonna beat the crap out of me for no reason at all.**

I've got no real idea why I got picked on and persecuted so much.

Jealousy is the only reason I can think of. I had a lot of male attention, and I guess these girls just didn't like that. I got jumped when I wasn't expecting it and I got beaten up at least another five times by gangs of girls and on one occasion had a bottle smashed over my head.

> To make it worse, my mum has suffered from Schizoaffective Disorder since I was born, which is a combination of Schizophrenia and Bipolar Disorder, so I didn't want her to see me with black eyes or whatever. Her symptoms included hearing voices, having dramatic mood swings and paranoia, and being highly emotional. Her episodes would bubble up during the year and she'd have to go into hospital for 1 to 4 months.

I would do what I could for her when I was there. My mum is such a beautiful, kind person and it's so hard watching her suffer, even though she's now on the right medication and is better than she's ever been. She is so strong and that is why she's my idol and I love

her very much. It's been tough, but when you grow up with it you learn how to deal with it.

That was this whole other worry waiting for me at home, so I never wanted to go home and be around that. It made me sad, so I would stay out and try not to worry her with my problems. She was very confused about the situation, didn't understand it, and she couldn't really have helped anyway. These kids had no respect for adults at all. They'd come to my house whether my mum was there or not and probably give her a kicking too if she tried to intervene. That was the extent of the violence.

My parents had been separated since I was nine and sometimes I would go and stay with my dad, but I'd keep the front up with him as well, playing it down as just a little scrap, and making out like I fought back, so he was none the wiser.

I internalised it all really. I'd spend every night in front of my mirror throwing punches and trying to come up with ways to defend myself. By this stage I just wanted my life back and to be left alone.

It was a very hard stage of my life and I became really depressed and started self-harming. I would sit in my room slicing up my arms with anything I could find, mainly scissors. It's really hard to explain why you self-harm. It was a way of expressing my pain, I suppose, and feeling something. I used to smash my head against the wall at night and cry my eyes out, begging God to give me a career in music so I could be happy. I was hurting myself off and on for a few years until I turned 16. No one really knew what I was up to because I was good at hiding it – wearing long sleeves and things.

It disturbs me when I think about it too much, even now.

FIGHT YOU AFTER SCHOOL!

As soon as I knew how to read and write and do some basic maths, I just didn't give a damn about anything else and I was a little rat.

From when I was 11 in Year Seven I just bunked all the time and headed for my dad's studio. That's what I was interested in. I was at three secondary schools and a Unit too. I was a naughty boy in dem days and school was just a joke ting to me.

My first secondary school was St Aloysius in Islington. I think I was there for about a year but I can't remember because I wasn't there that often. I got kicked out for fighting too much – that's all I really remember about it there.

Then when I was around 12 I went to Bishop Douglass School, and I got into a lot of fights there too so I was always getting suspended. In the end I got accused of something really bad – something I didn't do, and don't even want to talk about – and together with my fighting they used it to kick me out of there too. The fights were always over some sort of stupidness. People making fun out of me, or saying something behind my back, so I'd tell 'em, 'Come on then, after school', and a big crowd of people would gather.

I remember those fights would always start with someone hitting me while I wasn't looking and that's what'd make you lose the fight more often than not.

Funnily enough as a schoolboy it was people like Bruce Lee who I looked up to because he was always fightin' too! I've always been a fighter to tell you the truth – never will give up on nuttin'! I always had to stand up for myself, especially because I'm small. People would love to punch me in my face and then go and tell their friends the next day.

Then I went to Haverstock aged 12 or 13 and hooked up with Fazer and I just bunked it and bunked it and bunked it. Me and him just used to roll together everywhere all the time – and it's been like that since then.

I didn't actually get kicked out of Haverstock, I just stopped going, and that's why after a while I went to an Arts and Media Unit called WAC. I decided to just get a few grades under my belt and I got an A+ for English and a B for music. What else did I need for my career?!

I ain't gonna big up no teachers because it didn't feel like none of them gave a damn about me. As far as I'm concerned those schools never gave out no positivity. You didn't feel like you could come out and get a job or achieve anything from being there. They didn't give you that message – if anything it seemed like most of the teachers didn't want to be there themselves. And that meant school was just playtime to me.

Way I see it, in schools like that you're only going to get bad kids coming out. In posh private schools with kids wearing bags two feet thick full of books – that's where you're gonna get a good education. But we never had the money for that because we were in Camden and just had to make do.

Bun dat! Where we was it was just playtime. Some of the girls might TRY and go to a few lessons, but they'd end up getting drawn into whatever everyone else was doing.

Truth be told I haven't really got any happy memories that come from being in school. My school education was such a quick ting for me that it doesn't feature as a part of my life.

To be fair, though, I was always really popular, of course! At the first two schools I was known for being a bit of a little shit and certain kids might not like me, but at Haverstock I was proper popular. Me and Fazer was probably the most popular in the school, I would say.

I never really suffered from the classic awkward teenage stage to be honest. I was always confident and all that. If anything I spent a little bit of time thinking I was a bit too slim, a bit too skinny, but nah, man … just get on with life innit?!

As a young boy you wanna show off a lot. You wanna show who's got the best trainers, who's had the most fights, who's the first to get a moped and all that stuff. I was involved in that big time – but I got out of it.

I wasn't exactly a bully – maybe I was a bit harsh to a few kids a few times, but nah, I wasn't a bully and no one bullied me, no way. I did get beaten up a few times at my first school though, but always by boys that were bigger than me.

I'm really pissed off with myself that I never went to school and got a proper education. I'm pissed off that I didn't have that opportunity because of lack of money. Now I wanna tell kids to try and get as many different GCSEs and as many different bloomin' A-levels as possible.

Stay in school and do your work, I'm telling you. If I didn't have my music I'd be in trouble with my no qualifications. Because I know people who have got five GCSEs and a couple of A-levels and they're STILL finding it hard to get a job. Imagine if you have NONE of them!

You HAVE to get an education. HAVE TO. It gives you such a broader range of things available to you in life and stops you from being narrow-minded.

Learning gives you options and options are always good.

SCHOOL REPORTS

Name: ~~Nigel~~ Dappy

SUBJECT	REMARKS
First Nickname	Dappy - it comes from dapper. Because I've always been a dapper dude trying to accomplish something with my life.
Worst Subject	History and Geography Those two together - yuk! Could not care less!
Best Subject	English When I decided to go for my grades quickly English I just got. I like words.
Favourite School Meal	Casserole with gravy and meat and chips with it. Then whatever pudding they had.
Best School Trip	I went paintballing and ever since then I've wanted to go back and sneak about in the woods like a sniper.
Favourite Teacher	None Didn't like any of them - none of them liked me.

Name: Tulisa

SUBJECT
First Nickname
Worst Subject
Best Subject
Favourite School Meal
Best School Trip
Favourite Teacher

REMARKS

'T'. That's what I've always been known as right up until today.

Science. I just couldn't fathom it. I missed a few classes and the next thing I know they're talking about atoms and stuff!

Drama. I've always liked acting and it's something I still want to do more of.

Always loved school dinners. I love aeroplane food too. My favourite was chicken burger and chips.

We went to the Natural History Museum. I had an obsession with dinosaurs and wanted to be an archaeologist.

Miss Shield at Quintin Kynaston. She was the only one who tried to help me.

Name: **Fazer**

SUBJECT	REMARKS
First Nickname	Steppa or DJ Ricky B, I can't remember which but they both just sounded cool.
Worst Subject	English – even though I loved my teacher Mr Crocker it just wasn't for me.
Best Subject	Science – Playing with the Bunsen Burner was always fun I can't lie!
Favourite School Meal	Chocolate cake and chocolate custard every time :)
Best School Trip	Hmmm I was never allowed to go on any.
Favourite Teacher	Mr Crocker all the way and every time. Duku yourself, sir!

STREET LIFE

Life outside school and on the street taught me very different lessons from what school showed me. I learned to keep a very close circle of friends. I used to roll with up to 30 mates a day all in one crew. We used to hang around Swiss Cottage and group up outside KFC. That's when I got my nickname Fazer. It came about from my love of motorbikes. I had my little moped – my Gilera – and I loved it, doing wheelies everywhere and stuff. But some of my older friends had bigger bikes – one of them had a Yamaha Fazer and I just loved that bike. He'd let me borrow it every now and then and it was proper fast – so I just took that name because it suited me.

It goes to show you which of those are the REAL mates – because they're still around today. Know who your mates are. From that group there's no more than six of them still in my life. The others have gone their own ways.

I always say to my little brother to avoid all those goons and don't talk about your business or money matters with anyone. If someone's doing worse than you are, they don't want to see you doing well. Watch out for backstabbers.

Swiss Cottage is weird because the rich side and the hood side are split by just one road. Rich on one side, poor on the other. We were the only black family in a council flat on the nice side. Everyone else had bought their house and had a nice car – except us.

FAZER

I grew up there, but I always crossed the other side of the road to the hood. That's where I spent my time – on the Kilburn side or the Camden side. Because when I spent any time on my road there was that racism thing again. When I walked down my road, people would look at me funny. If my mates came around, the police would get called for no reason just because they were outside my house.

At the time I was growing up, the area had the highest number of mentally unstable people in the country living there. And there were drugs everywhere. Crackheads all over the place and heroin too – it was really in your face and a part of daily life.

I didn't have money. My mum did some cash-in-hand work and my dad would put up market stalls at the weekend – I needed to make money of my own. But I also wanted to do my music, so I didn't want to go and work nine to five or behind a counter. I tried working at a flower stall in Camden but they didn't pay me enough so I started nicking 50-pound notes every day. They'd pay me 20 quid for the day and I'd top it up from the till with a couple of pinkies. They never found me out, but I knew that wasn't the future for me.

And when you see people running around making a quick buck selling weed and drugs and you don't have more than a couple of quid in your pocket, it's tempting. How could I go into town with no more than a bus fare? I did dabble with getting involved with that scene, but I broke away from it.

N-Dubz really led me away from that. I had something creative to put my effort into and I started making a little money too.

My whole life was going into the studio from 13 onwards.

I was there all the time. But in between I was signing on too and trying to get work. I did try, but I wanted a job in music. That was my dream and I didn't want to do anything else.

I pursued it and it led me out. I can't say the same for a lot of my friends who aren't here right now. Some of them are doing long prison sentences, others have been deported and a couple of them have been killed.

I even got stabbed back in the day – just above my belly. It happens if you're out there. I don't mind if people know this – hopefully they can learn from it so it won't happen to them.

I was walking to the studio one day a few years ago and a guy with his hood up came up and asked me if I had the time. I took out my phone and told him the time and the next minute he had a knife to me and told me to give him my phone.

We had a scuffle and luckily I was able to fend him off, even though he managed to cut me just below my chest. Looking back on it I know that I shouldn't have put up any resistance. I wouldn't advise anyone to try and play the hero – no possession is worth dying for.

After that I got robbed at gunpoint. I was driving my car and three or four youngsters ran up to my window when I stopped at the lights. The next thing I knew, one of them had leaned in and ripped my chain off my neck. I jumped out and chased after them until one of them turned around and started shooting at me! I couldn't believe it. I thought, 'Nah – I'm not dying for this.' I got back in my car, drove away and never thought about that chain again. Don't die for something stupid – that's a message I want to get across to people. Especially if you're out there on the streets when things DO happen.

The knife-crime problem was blowing up around the same time that we were and I feel strongly about it. I'm anti-knives 100 per cent. Don't walk out with a knife. And definitely leave the guns alone too. One knife or bullet goes around 22 people.

It's a vicious cycle of actions and reactions. If you stab someone, his mate's gonna come back and stab you, then your mate's gonna shoot him AND his mate and it escalates until there's untold people involved. All over something stupid.

Get rid of the problem before it even starts – don't carry a knife. If someone's giving you grief, use your fists if you have to do something. You don't need to use a knife.

Even though I'm a hothead myself, I know you have to try and think first before you act. If you have a knife on you and you get scared, you won't think, you'll just use it.

I took my little brother on tour with me last year and it might have saved his life. When he's back home he always hangs around with his mate H – they're together all the time. H got stabbed while he was away. My little brother would have been there and most likely got stabbed too if it wasn't for that tour.

Even so, growing up, I never liked the police. They made my teenage years a misery. I would get stopped and searched three or four times a day and they even raided my house for no reason at all. They'd go through my

mum's personal stuff with some stupid excuse. I used to tell certain ones of them to take their uniform off and come and meet me without your badge and we'll have a scuffle and then see. I was 16 and these big men would act like bullies. I didn't like them at all. It was the way they treated me that caused the problem.

> They do serve a purpose for some people and some things.
> If my house ever got robbed now, I would call them to get a crime reference number and for insurance purposes, but that's it. They won't do anything to help me. It shouldn't be like that, but that's the reality and I have to deal with that.

Their service is supposed to stop people breaking the law but they're the biggest law-breakers around.

> It would be a mad world if there were no police in it, and they do keep some things in check, but things need to change. Like with teachers, they need to work WITH people and not work against people by labelling them and stereotyping them. That's what makes people hate the law and feel okay about breaking it.

> Even now I get stopped in my car. I'll be driving and they'll just assume I'm a drug dealer or something like that. I tell them straight, 'I'm not a drug dealer, my face is on TV!'

Once I had a couple of grand cash on me and they took it off me, telling me I couldn't have that sort of cash unless I could prove where it came from. If I was a white man in a business suit driving in my BMW that would never happen. How can I not be allowed to have money from legal sources just because I'm young and black?

They made me go to the police station with receipts just so I could reclaim my own money. That's madness.

It's still going on now. And even now, if I get stopped and searched I STILL give the wrong name and address. It's not like I've got warrants out on my name or anything but it's just habit and how they make me feel.

I have to say I think I had to grow up too quickly. By the time I was 16, I was 16 going on 27. That's not how it should be. You should be enjoying your youth, going to the cinemas, going to clubs and doing the stuff kids do. You should enjoy your innocence.

I had a great family but we never had much money, and it's worrying about money that makes you grow up quick. I started knocking around with some of the bad boys doing stuff to make a quick buck at a young age, and that took away my innocence. But I was able to step away from that when they couldn't, because I loved my music more than anything. The drive I had to succeed and go to another level as a musician took me away from anything that could endanger that.

I always believed in N-Dubz from the day we started – mainly because we had Dappy's dad believing in us the whole time. He was our motivator.

FIGHTING BACK

Aged about 15 I fell in with a new, older group of girls around Camden who were more serious faces. Then things really changed for me and I went down a bad path. But it had its positives.

As a part of this group of girls I wasn't a person that was messed with anymore. There were about 20 of us and we had a reputation that people were afraid of. We would go around getting into all sorts of trouble, starting on people for no reason, having big fights with groups of girls from other areas. We were just this aggressive gang of chicks out to cause mayhem.

I guess a lot of the girls in the gang felt irrelevant and powerless in life and that was our way of empowering ourselves. And for me, it was a different buzz. Like when I had first become popular at school I got a real buzz from people liking me, but now I was getting it from people being scared of me and my associates.

That's how I got the courage to start standing up for myself. When I'd been getting beaten up in the past, I would just cower, cover myself and take the beatings.

But now I was the bully. I was hitting people and for me that was better than getting my head kicked in.

I remember there being a lot of weapons about too. Knives are a bad thing but what we really need to look at is why people carry them in the first place. Of course a heavy jail sentence is good because it will scare people off taking weapons out, but it won't stop the problem. We need to sort the kids out before they get to that stage.

I believe kids today have big problems and it's all about empowerment.

Celebs on TV are seen as the ultimate way to be. That's what you must achieve. But not everyone can have that life, and seeing all the glitz and glamour can just make people feel less relevant. If they can't achieve all that, then the only way they can get power or respect is through violence on the street.

The same buzz I get from a crowd screaming my songs, some of these kids will get from hurting other people. Because so many of them have failed with education, they can't get satisfaction from succeeding in a positive way with good marks and then later, good jobs.

I think a lot of it has to do with the parents and the schools. If you catch children young enough they won't go down the wrong route. I feel that some parents might even need to have classes on how to raise their children these days. If parents have certain mind-frames and negative energies, they pass it down to their kids and they think it's okay to behave badly too. If kids aren't disciplined enough by their parents they won't respect them, and they'll have no one to look up to. Morals and chivalry have gone out of the window.

I hate to think what it's going to be like in 40 years' time.

Teachers should be allowed to give out more discipline. Generations ago kids would get the cane or a wallop at school and they were too scared to mess about and not do their work. We need some of that back now. We need to give kids a firm hand. Teachers should be strong as well as being good at teaching and give the kids someone to respect and look up to.

I would have been a better person back then if I had had a better school life.

Looking back, I'm not proud of the things I did in that stage of my life and if I could take back any of the hurt I caused I would. But I can't. And everything happens for a reason anyway and it's made me the person I am. Plus most of the girls we were fighting were just as aggressive and nasty as us – it was bad on bad.

In one way I was lucky to fall in with that group because I learned to stand up for myself and I was never bullied or victimised again, but I can't recommend that sort of behaviour to other people. Luckily we all grew up to be good people.

If you're getting bullied and you've got someone you can talk to about what's going on, who can help you, make sure you do. Otherwise try and keep yourself to yourself, and be as aware as you can of the negative people or troublemakers so you can stay away from them. Try and stand up for yourself if they pick on you, but if it's too much and the teachers can't sort it out, then move schools.

After my year out, I moved schools again and went to Quintin Kynaston. I'd been with my new group of friends for a while, so my confidence was up and no one messed with me anymore. I never wanted to experience that feeling of being weak again, so I was up for anything with anyone who wanted to start. I wasn't horrible, but I was very defensive and ready for trouble.

In terms of education, though, there was really no point in me being there. I was cocky and there was nothing any teacher there could say that I wanted to listen to. Apart from Miss Shield, who was the only teacher that I respected. She cared for me as a kid and wanted me to do the best that I could do at school. If I bunked she came to my house to try and get me into school.

She gave me a bit of hope and made me feel like I wasn't worthless. The more teachers were dismissive of me, the more I would rebel, whereas she took the other approach. Because deep down I was a nice person, when she was nice to me I couldn't be a bitch to her. She got my friendship. If I'd had more teachers like her I would have been much better at school. As it was, I would just go into class and either go to sleep or I'd listen to my iPod. I was probably one of the worst students in the school.

I do regret not getting a proper education – but at the time I was so sure I was going to be a singer that I felt I didn't need it. Now, I love knowledge and learning and I do want to try and better my education as much as possible. I do wish I had more of that about me then.

I wasn't really happy at all as a teenager and I even started getting into witchcraft. Someone showed me some Tarot cards and I started looking into spiritualism. I saw it all as another form of empowerment. I saw a movie about teenage witches and thought it would be so cool to be able to cast spells and that kind of thing.

I bought loads of books about it, which led to another weird stage of my life as I started having really weird spiritual experiences around me. I tried using a Ouija board and I believe I brought something bad out. Things would start moving in my house or the bed would start shaking. No joke!

I remember sitting with Fazer telling him there was a dark energy following me around. He told me I was actually going mad and started laughing. I told him it was in the room right now and, as I said it, the lights switched off and the radio came blaring on. He was terrified.

I would have dreams in the night and make predictions in them which would come true over the next few days. I dreamed that my mate was face down in a bathtub with blood pouring out of her head and she was just floating lifeless in it with a cracked skull. Two days after that dream she got run over by a car, cracked her head open and was in a coma for two weeks.

TULISA

Plus I was seeing reflections of a man looking at me through a window, hearing footsteps and having nightmares of spirits and demons. I thought I was seriously going mad.

But I was pulled out of that phase by rediscovering my faith. I started having religious dreams. I dreamed that Mother Mary came and spoke to me. She told me that she watches over me and when I cry she cries too – pretty deep, I know. Other religious icons came to me in my dreams too and told me that I needed to leave these negative energies behind. They told me to pray, and that praying would save me and take away all the dark energy and bring me back to the light.

I started praying again and returned to the belief and faith that I had as a child. The dreams stopped, the dark feelings went away and it really did help me find my normal self again.

I even got a job. I wanted to make a bit of money for myself on the side so I got my first job in a hairdresser's. But I quit that after not too long because all I wanted to know about was music.

I was able to get a job in the music industry via a friend of my auntie's. I was a receptionist at a music-management company called Sanctuary. It was only a small place, but we did The Who and Led Zeppelin, so it was a big job with lots of responsibility. But even then I was getting so involved in my music that I soon started slacking off the work and making mistakes or coming in with a hangover. In the end we went our separate ways because I forgot to post off a £40,000 cheque! It was a good experience but it also made me realise how much I never wanted to be in an office.

NAUGHTINESS

If I weren't in N-Dubz, the honest truth is I would not be in a good position now. First of all, my dad's gone and he always used to give me a lot of guidance when I was doing naughty stuff on the street and getting in trouble.

I'd say I'd be either dead or in jail. One of the two if I never did music. Straight up DEAD OR IN JAIL.

There's no way I'd be in no nine to five job. I would never be able to have a boss tell me what to do. And yeah, that most probably is a little bit of a failure on my part. I'll be honest, my mum thinks I need to go and get a bit of counselling because I'm a bit everywhere, a bit all over the shop. One minute I'm happy, the next minute I'm sad, then I'm all aggro and wanna do something naughty – you get me, I'm not easy.

Outside of school is where I learned right from wrong – and that's a massive thing in life. You're capable of doing anything in life with your two hands and your brain. And the best way to learn right from wrong is to experience it through your own actions. You learn if you do this then you're gonna get in trouble, but if you do that then you're gonna go in the right direction.

DAPPY

If you do both of them you learn double fast. When I was a teenager I was getting up to all sorts to make money, and then I had a scare. I realised that I could go to prison for years of my life. To go from that to now, making legitimate money as an upstanding citizen, I can really see how I'm supposed to be. Behaving badly doesn't have a future for anyone, behaving well benefits the future of the whole community.

Someone who's had everything in life from the very start won't necessarily be able to see the difference between right and wrong so clearly. If you've had a big house, big dis, big dat, car home anytime, £100 in your pocket to go out shopping my little darling! Bun dat. You got a great life, but you don't really know life.

It's funny how boys who grew up like that wanna try and be like us – like people who grew up where we did. They listen to hip-hop and go on like they're bad, wearing all the clothes and chains. And it's all come from their dad's money. And it's funny how we wanna try and be like they are!

That's why anyone who doesn't have to get into naughtiness on the street, be it selling drugs, robbing houses or whatever, should NEVER do it. It's not cool and the reason people are doing that is because they have to. We wanna try and get what you already have.

I'm thankful for the background I have, and that's why I still know all dem man from back in the day and I still know what's going on in my area.

Because knowing what was wrong has made it easier for me to see what's right. And that learning doesn't come from any school in the world.

Look, my area weren't Iraq. Bloomin' 'ell – there weren't people dying every second or nothing like that, but a lot of spiteful, bad things would happen there. It was a very negative environment to grow up in. I've seen some truly horrible, gruelling things and those things have changed me as a person. They've made me blunt to some things.

I mean – I saw legs in a bin bag. Smelt them and seen the blue skin where the bag was torn. That was at the end of my block of flats. The Camden Ripper had dumped these two bodies there. I was 13 when I saw that and since then I started growing up quick. When you see that kind of thing it makes an impression on you.

Where I grew up you just got hard quickly and used anything you could to get by, because that's what other people would do to you.

DAPPY

We used to sit in the KFC in Swiss Cottage – a big crew of us, all rowdy – like little rats, making the guy behind the counter give us free chicken and chips. We'd see how much we could convince him to give us to make us leave.

In my mid- to late teens, that was when the most crazy stuff was happening in my life. A lot of my friends went to jail for doing stupidness and getting caught. Just to be the big man with the most bucks.

Which brings me to the police! I still struggle to look at them in a positive way – because of their attitude towards me and my friends as youngsters growing up in a bad environment. They know that if we were financially stable as youths, we wouldn't have been doing these naughty things on the street. But they don't see it as a problem, they see it as a game. They liked seeing us as bad guys and had fun making our lives hell when we were just trying to make ends meet using the cards we had been dealt.

Now some people will read this and think that makes me a narrow-minded little plonker, but those people probably never had to survive like I did and they don't know what they would have done in my situation.

I would get stopped and searched all the time just for they way I looked. Even if I wasn't doing anything wrong they would be on top of me, making my day-to-day life hard, just because I had a hat and a hoody on.

But up to this day the police still make it hard for me to say positive things about them because they STILL trouble me.

I'm an upstanding, working man with legitimate money and my own business to run and they still stop me because of how I look. Only difference is now I'm in my car and they pull me over rather than stop me on the street. The other thing that's really changed is they recognise me most times now.

They're like 'I saw you on *Jonathan Ross*, I saw you on *Buzzcocks* ...' and I give them a high five and we have a little chinwag and it's all friendly. But that's just because I'm famous.

Just last week two of them saw my rolled-up cigarette and assumed it was a spliff. Two hours they had me standing there going on like I had committed some sort of crime or something. It's the only time in my life I've wanted to say, 'Don't you know who I am, bruv?!'

But in general, these days, I do my best to be civil with them and it often turns out their daughters or sons are fans and they wanna get a little autograph or something.

One of those coppers was even a fan himself! We were promoting our first album in Brent Cross in London, and one of them came up to us and started rapping our lyric about police from 'Ouch' to us ... I felt good about that.

Apart from police, I was always – ALWAYS – respectful of adults. Every time.

That's one thing I made sure of was to be a bloomin' real genuine person with manners to adults and they will like you. Anyone will tell you. I might be a little rat, but when it comes to adults you have to be respectful and show them some courtesy.

These days it's like kids get more respect out of being disrespectful to their elders. Of course we've all done that up to a certain level, but when it matters, you have to treat them with respect. I used to be shit scared of my mum and my dad when I was growing up as a little kid and that stuck with me.

My mum and dad brought me up in a beautiful home environment – in the very best way they could. They always had love for me, they were always there for me. It was just financially difficult – that's all that was lacking in my upbringing. We lived in a little shoebox on a dirty little estate – that's what I called it: the shoebox. But inside the flat it was great. It was homely and a wonderful environment despite being so small.

Bang! The moment you step outside that front door it's a negative environment again. Sometimes there was nights where my mum would be crying and begging me not to go out, but I ignored her. I wanted to be able to get my own money and pay for my own things. Be able to show my mum – look, this is what I have got. But I didn't really see that I was making her into an emotional wreck because I would get into trouble with the police over some of the things I did.

I got arrested so many times that it was almost a joke. I got caught for a lot of minor things, but they start to add up as previous and then become a big thing. As I've said in one of my songs, my lawyer is a magician for keeping me out of prison.

Mainly, I had love from my mum and my dad, and that's what made me drag myself up out of being a little shit out on the streets doing badness. I wanted to make them proud and I didn't wanna make my mum cry any more. She used to weep and say, 'You're not like this, I didn't raise you to be this person.'

The goodness and softness about me comes down to love from my family, and the badness comes from where I grew up and money, money, money. I had to wise up. If I'd had an education, that's the time I would have been coming out with A-levels and going for a job to earn a living. But I didn't. I had my music, and so I pursued that harder than anything and put the street life to one side.

DAPPY
ON GIRLS

I first started getting interested in girls when I was 12. **Blam!** Straight away. I've had two serious girlfriends in my life and the first one was when I was 14. I don't wanna say her name, but I was with her for three or four years and she was my friend as well as my girlfriend.

I must admit — I have always been successful with girls. I am taken now, but the thing is I was always just comfortable with girls. I never felt that any girl was going to turn me down, so I would always just bowl up and talk to any girl who caught my eye. It didn't matter if they were tall, short, skinny, whatever ... I just always knew how to talk to them.

It's mad to think that some people see me as a heart-throb though. It's just me innit?!

Funny thing is, I didn't chase my missus Kaye — she found me! She knew someone who knew someone who knew me and she managed to get my number. We spoke on the phone for ages over about two weeks. We started looking at each other on the internet and then finally I went over to where she was living to meet her and she was so shy. When she eventually sat down next to me I just looked at her for ages, drinking her in. I couldn't take my eyes off her — and now, two and a half years later, here we are!

But my advice to the lads who haven't got a girlfriend is pretty simple. The best way to catch a girl's attention is to make sure you're surrounded by girls already. That let's them know you're a good guy and they can relax around you. Plus they'll be curious. Keep up plenty of eye contact and keep smiling. Let them know that you're just as much of a catch as they are and if they don't wanna talk to you, it's their loss as much as yours.

When you get chatting, make them laugh and be real with them. Get a feel for what they're like, but be wary! I once had a terrible experience with a girl a few years ago. She was hot, but when I put my hand on her back I felt the biggest, hairiest mole in the world. I had to make my excuses and leave quick time.

For me, the ideal woman has to be from the hood 'cos she'll keep you grounded, not like some famous or rich chick, but each to his own!

The best place to take them for a first date is McDonald's. Go straight there like me and my missus Kaye. Then, try to impress the girlfriend's parents the first time you meet them by showing them that you are clever, well-mannered and can hold a conversation.

Be romantic with her as best you can. My most romantic gesture was probably buying Kaye a beautiful candle-lit dinner in Barbados overlooking the beach and watching the sun set.

You don't have to go that far, but even the little things are noticed.

Trust me, lads!

PART 2
FIRST TASTE OF SUCCESS

TWO TURNTABLES AND A MICROPHONE

Dappy came to my school when we were about 12 and we started hanging out. He got kicked out of about four schools for fighting and that. I was writing lyrics to Garage then – when it was all still TwoStep – and one day Dappy told me he wrote a lyric. Then he spat these few lyrics and he was boom! Before then Dappy used to just come and sing songs when we were chilling and play air guitar from old-school tunes.

Me and Dappy always used to clash each other. That's how we got good – by bouncing off each other. We would battle and then go home and write more lyrics to try and beat each other's lyrics so it was always a little competitive edge.

At that time, I had two belt-drive turntables in my house so we would start writing lyrics over tunes more and more. We would try and do two-hour tapes as if we were a pirate radio station. We'd go for hours.

Dappy and me used to just be out in the area and we would clash some of the MCs already on the radio out on the street for fun. We were calling ourselves Likkle Rinsers Crew – LRC.

After a while we gatecrashed one of SLK's radio sets – they were local to us – we just turned up one day. We brought a couple of mates just in case they didn't want us there! The only danger was my little bit of nerves. There were loads of people all around this room and a circle of people spitting on the mic. I got passed the mic and pow – straight in to do my thing then pass it to Dappy, then back to me, then back to him. We gatecrashed the whole set and we were so tight because we'd been practising in my bedroom for so much time. We knew how it was supposed to sound.

Off the back of that, the guy that owned the station told us we should come and do a weekly set and properly tear it up. We had to pay to do it, but we did every Thursday night and just kept improving our lyrics and mastering our art.

It cost us £15 a week to use their equipment and set-up, which was a lot to us back then, but we were happy to spend it. I was on the radio, with people listening to me and Dappy's lyrics and texting in – that was a good feeling. We had a slot on Flair FM, then we went to Flex FM for a bit and we did a lot on Y2K as well.

We were still only 13 or 14 but we wanted to make records even then. Dappy's dad had a studio in Dollis Hill and Dappy said we could probably use it. So we went in with DJ Deekline – who did 'I Don't Smoke Da Reefa' – because we had an idea for a song. It was called 'What Is This World Coming To, We Don't Give a Fuck'. That was how we felt at the time – like young rebels.

But now me and Dappy were trying to work out who we could get to sing. There was a girl in school called Rachel who was supposed to do it, but she didn't turn up at the studio. Then Dappy said: 'Let me try my cousin – she sings. Maybe she'll do it.'

So we got Dappy's dad to go to Tulisa's house and ask her to come and be on a song with her cousin. She turned him down because she wanted to be a solo artist! But Dappy's dad gave her £20 and she changed her mind! She was only 11 or 12 at the time and since then, it's been us. We haven't looked back.

The first track we did that sounded like a full song was 'What Is This World Coming To?'. We were so proud of that because it sounded like a proper record even though we were still just kids. From there we just developed our different roles in the group – with me and Dappy playing Dumb and Dumber!

Dappy is like a motivator for the band. He'll ring me up and tell me, 'Fazer – you need to come to the studio today. I won't be there but you need to get some beats ready for this, that and the other.' Without him, sometimes I can be a bit of a couch potato.

But we all play a very strong part within this group. When it comes to vocals me and Dappy are like tag-team partners, and Dappy is probably one of the best vocal engineers in the country. He doesn't even know it. He's got a proper ear for a good vocal. He'll spend hours going through take after take to find the perfect one. Dappy's job is the vocals man.

When we're in the studio, if people are a bit down it's me who brings the atmosphere up – that's my job. If Tulisa and Dappy have had one of their arguments I'm the one that steps in and says 'Look, dash that, man, we got a record to do.' Then we can just leave all bullshit aside and make a smashing record.

The thing is, because Dappy and Tulisa are cousins and they grew up together – same area, same family and that – when they have a fight it's like brother and sister. I'm just like the middle man who has to step in and reason with both of them. That's what makes the records what they are – the arguments that we have in the studio are a crucial part of pushing until we get the best possible sound that everyone is happy with.

Tulisa's role comes in a lot when we're on the road, doing press stuff, interviews, TV all day. Me and Dappy have a bit of a short attention span, so we'll both start wandering off and doing mad stuff to keep ourselves entertained. That's when Tulisa will come in and say, 'Look, we're in a public place now, we've got a job to do, you can't be acting like this, you're making yourself look stupid.' She'll give us a little ticking off because she's like the mother hen of the group.

And we'll take that from her. That's T, that's how she is. Some of the stuff that she says to us, if it was another girl it would be a different story. The way we ALL talk to each other – if we were a group put together by a record label instead of friends, we would have split by now.

And the thing is, N-Dubz could never work if one of us was to leave. We couldn't just replace someone, like the Sugababes. We could all go and do something on a solo trip, but when us three are together, magic happens. There's a mad chemistry between us and we are all grateful to be involved in something so unique.

We all have different musical tastes too. In terms of my early influences people would be surprised. I used to listen to stuff like Aretha Franklin, Bessie Smith, John Lee Hooker, Billie Holiday, The Mavericks, Elvis, Eddie Cochran and loads of Motown. Maybe not what people would expect, but that's what my mum and dad were into, so I was listening to that kind of thing as I was growing up. But my whole life changed when I heard swearing in music for the first time. It was hip-hop. When I heard Wu Tang for the first time. That album – *36 Chambers* – I couldn't believe it. I was hearing swear words in music. I was like 'Whoooooah!' Those days I was playing Mario Kart on the Super Nintendo and listening to Wu and it was all good! That was me for days!

You can still hear the hip-hop influences in my rhymes.

NO DOUGH, NO SHOW

When I was 11 Dappy and Fazer asked me to come and join them to make a track in the studio. Dappy was already spitting and Fazer was rapping and dj-ing too, but they needed a singer.

I remember me being all snooty and saying I wanted to be a solo artist, why should I be on your track? I said no, so they asked this other girl from school – who said yes but then never showed up. The first I knew of it was my Uncle Byron was at my house asking me to come and sing on a track with the boys. He offered me £20, and then when I said no he made it a pinky. So I said yes!

I went down and we recorded our first ever song – 'What Is This World Coming To?'. Dappy was fiddling on the keyboard and Fazer was playing around with some instruments too and they were trying to produce their first little track. It was hilarious really and if anyone was to hear it now they'd crack up. But to me it sounded like a song. I was an 11-year-old with a song – no matter how crap it was! From that day forward we've been together.

We decided to call ourselves the Likkle Rinsers because we were only little but we still rinsed it. Lol. Dappy came up with the name after pissing himself laughing at my corny idea – I wanted to call us the BOOM Crew!

When you're that young in the studio there are no nerves. You just go with the flow. As a young girl I was very into Aaliyah, 112, Boyz II Men, Monica, and older R&B that my friend's older sisters were listening to. But in terms of influences 'One in a Million' by Aaliyah really stands out as an early one. And I wanted to be a solo star like her. I was singing in the school playground and singing on the street with my friends or to anyone that would listen, but that was it.

I thought of myself as a singer though. From the first time I was in my school play as Tallulah in *Bugsy Malone*. At breaktime people would just crowd around me and I would sit and sing songs people requested. It was just T singing time and my mates would sit and listen to me.

It's funny how from those early days of me singing and us getting together, the three of us have developed as a group. Dappy is very much the obvious frontman. He wants and loves the fame as much as anything else. He loves the stage, being in the limelight and being the man of the moment.

Fazer is very chilled out. He's happy to just spit a verse on a track and then sit back and be the producer making the beats. He's like a Timbaland kind of figure.

I'm kind of a mix of the two of them. Sometimes I like to chill and be more laid-back than Dappy. I don't want the fame as much, but I do want the music as much as he does and I'm just as ambitious as him. Sometimes I just want to take the stage by storm and bust it up and overshadow Dappy – but other times I lean on him.

More often than not it's the boys who are the dopey ones and say the silly things. Dappy will say something and everyone will gasp. He's just eccentric and he'll say stupid things just to shock people. He's a proper nutta!

Fazer is the chilled joker and sometimes quite goofy. You can't hold a conversation with him for long because he just phases out and you have to shout his name about five times to get his attention.

I'm the mother hen, always shouting and moaning at everyone and telling them what to do. I have to keep the boys in check and boss them about. I try and manage their lives for them sometimes!

They're still young lads, and they have a lot of life to exerience yet, so I focus a lot of energy on trying to guide them.

TULISA'S MATTERS OF THE HEART

My first boyfriend was called Carlos. We went out for a good year and we're still friends to this day, but that was kind of innocent stuff.

I had my first proper boyfriend in an adult way a couple of years later. We were sexually active and I was staying over at his house. It was a bad relationship though.

I had lied about my age and he was older than me. He was really handsome and everyone fancied him, but he was violent and abusive towards me. He would also often leave me for another girl and then come back when he was bored of her. And I would always take him back.

It was mad because on the streets I was powerful and tough at this point, but as a female in a relationship, I was weak as hell. He just broke me down into nothing and made me feel like crap. He'd tell me I was ugly and lock me in the bathroom while he went out. But I don't blame him – he had a very tough upbringing and was a bit of a lost child at the time. It was just unfortunate that I got the backlash of it. I think he's sorted himself out now. He just needed help.

Eventually he left me for another girl and I was so devastated that I stopped eating and dropped a stone and a half down to seven stone. That's when the self-harming got really bad and I even took it further twice by trying to kill myself.

I went to the next level with it. My mum obviously had loads of different kinds of pills in her cupboard, so I went in there and grabbed a bottle of whatever I could see. I didn't know what was what so I just ended up necking a load of pills and then becoming really sick and throwing up. Another time I slashed my wrists and they started bleeding really badly, which panicked me as I realised what I was doing to myself. I remember just sitting there holding a towel over it and crying, thinking what am I doing and hoping I hadn't managed to cut into a vein.

It really was a bad time for me. When he left I was so desperate to be loved by a man that I went off the rails for a while – 90 per cent of any sexual experiences I've ever had were within a year of the break-up. I can still count them on my fingers, but because it was in such a short space of time it felt like a lot. But I so badly wanted a boyfriend. I wanted to feel love and security, so I would date them for a while and then let them sweet-talk me into sleeping with them. They would say how lovely I was and that they'd never hurt me, that they'd stick around, and then they'd disappear. And it happened again and again. And the funny thing is I never enjoyed sex. I would go somewhere afterwards and cry, because I hated it so much. I think deep down I knew they were assholes, but for me it was always about just having someone hold me and give me a cuddle. But these guys were all older than me and just manipulated me, and it made me get even more depressed so I packed that in. I finally realised the deal, and after that year I began to love myself again, and that changed me. Now I could only have sex with someone that I see a future with and not just for some temporary affection. I can't just do it for attention – hence why I've only had two partners in the past five years.

The next year I met my ex, who I was with for a couple of years. We even got engaged. When we first met he was a player, but he hung around and gave me the attention I needed. It just became long-term and I only wanted one person in my life, so it worked for me. It was all light hearted in the beginning, but I was cool with that, because I just wanted male company.

But gradually I started to discover a bit of self-worth as I found my faith and got further and further away from the dark times. I was less willing to take his playing about and I think that may have made me more appealing to him because that's when he packed in the crap and we got together properly. We got engaged as a mutual decision on a random drunk night when I was 19, but to be realistic it was just a façade. I always felt there was something not right about us as a couple, but we were just in the groove and it was an easy thing to do.

Without going into too much detail we just were not right for each other, so we split up. People said it was because I cheated on him. Well that's just totally untrue. It's so far from being part of my character it's unbelievable. If I have someone, I don't need anyone else. I'm not a sexually oriented person.

I will say this though – I came out of that as a righteous person. It ended due to personal issues.

I was 21 by now, fully empowered as a woman, looking to buy my first house, and I finally felt like I didn't need a man at all. But I started talking on MySpace to an old crush called Justin (aka Ultra). We'd dated a while back, when me and my ex were broken up, but it didn't work at the time. But this time was different. We chatted for ages and then swapped numbers again and got friendly.

One thing led to another and suddenly we were a proper couple. Within three weeks of us meeting up again we went on holiday together because we just clicked so well. We were both much more grown-up than we had been when we had dabbled in the past and there was no game-playing or messing about.

Finally, this feels right. For the first time ever it feels like a completely comfortable and trusting relationship that's equal on both sides. It's my first time of being in love as a love should be.

Ultimately, I have grown so much as a woman that I no longer need to have imitations of love. I no longer feel irrelevant, like I'm trying to fill an empty gap. I'm complete and I'm with someone because I want to be, not because I feel I need to. That for me is real love, and I'm happy I've found it.

LITTLE STAR

Me and Fazer first met at karate when we were like seven or something. We were doing that on Saturdays as proper likkle yoots and we just used to tussle and that. We knew who each other was from the area and that, but until we started doing all that karate stuff we never really spoke much.

Then I started going to hang out at Fat David's house on Fazer's road and I remember Fazer used to come running in wearing his Man Utd T-shirt and with his dreadlocks flying everywhere. He was always hyper back then screaming 'Come we go blah blah, come let's blah blah…' – always with some plan. And the thing I remember most about Fazer as a kid was he ALWAYS smelled of juice. He always had some fresh diluted juice and I'd always want some of it.

So before I started going to the studio with Fazer, I wasn't really into the pop charts and that, I was just running around being a little kid and playing football and stuff. My only memory of tunes was because I would hear a lot of the music my dad would be playing, and I remember Heart 106.2 was always on the radio.

And the first time I ever picked up a mic was down to my dad. I was proper young – about nine – and I think it was around the time Craig David was coming out with Artful Dodger. My dad came into the room with a mic attached to a little tape recorder and played some Craig David. He was like: 'I've been hearing this thing, this sound – here … take this, chat for me!' and left me to it.

I had never even thought about it before at all but I gave it a go and I made this little rap for him on a tape deck. I played it to him and he started clapping and smiling and shouting 'Yes my son!' And since that time I KNEW I was gonna be a little star. After that I was just playing around with rapping and spitting a little bit on the streets.

Truth is, Fazer taught me how to MC. But now we do our different things. I'm more the MC now and Fazer does the track, but he will still spit a bar, because he can do it – and better than most too.

When my dad brought T to the studio that first time to sing with me and Fazer it was a joke ting. She turned up all aloof because she wanted to be a solo artist, and then she started singing through her nose, sounding all childish. She's come on since then, luckily.

Our first tune was called 'What Is This World Coming To?' – I'm embarrassed to even say that name, but hey, we was likkle yoots and it was still a tune anyway. I knew from when I heard that song coming back at us out of the speakers that we were gonna make some sick tunes in the future.

That's where the journey began as musicians and we developed ourselves from there to where you see us now. We just spent those first few years in the studio learning our craft. We knew what sound we wanted to go for – it was just a matter of developing ourselves to be able to achieve the level that we were happy with.

That unique N-Dubz sound that is so immediately recognisable now, we knew we wanted that, but we didn't know how to get to it.

We started out as Likkle Rinsers, but we soon changed to NW1 because that was our area code and we were all about bigging up where we came from. But then we thought actually nah – we're bigger than that, we're all over north-west London. So we dropped the one and became N-Dubz – Dubz as in W.

People refused to take us seriously for a long time in those early days because we were just three little kids with little rat voices. There were loads of times when all three of us thought we weren't gonna make it and that people weren't gonna be singing along to our lyrics like we thought they were.

Nowadays, me and Fazer don't battle each other no more like we did when were learning to spit in the old days. But every now and then if one of us does something stupid we will still cuss each other in a little rap or something – even T.

But if one of us three was to leave the band, we would no longer be N-Dubz. It's us three or nothing as a group. T could go and do a little solo thing, or I could just go out as Dappy with Fazer making beats for me, but there's no N-Dubz if one of us goes missing. That's why when I did

'Number One' with Tinchy Stryder I made sure it wasn't Tinchy Stryder feat Dappy, it was Tinchy Stryder feat N-Dubz. I want Tulisa and Fazer to be in the video too. Anytime I mention my name, I mention Tulisa and Fazer's too. That's how it is.

T is the mother hen. She'll always try and stop us from getting in trouble. We are very edgy and always very hyped, so she will try and keep a lid on us, make sure we don't overstep the mark, get me?

Fazer always has the tunes. Anything you here from us – it's him who's made that music. He's very smart mentally. He's the don of maths. And property too. When it comes to property I will always take his advice. Man's proper smart and intelligent and I listen to a lot of things he has to tell me. He leaves all the writing to me and I just sit back and watch with my mouth open wide when he gets involved with the computers and that to make our music.

Tulisa keeps us in check. But we have to keep her in check as well sometimes! I always tell T that there's more work to do. She sometimes goes on like we've done enough and can have a little break now, sit back and relax a bit.

But we don't see it like that. Me and Fazer's motto is 'You have to keep on working.' We always need to get another No. 1, another smash, another big show. I understand how she feels, but nah – no time for no relaxing business just yet!

DAPPY

On my right forearm I simply have Dappy and ND for N-Dubz tattooed on with some beautiful bandana patterns around it. That's my first tattoo and I got it in Camden maybe five years ago.

On my neck I've got RIP Dad, which speaks for itself — I had that done after my dad passed.

On my left forearm I have 2LISA for my cousin T. But I'm gonna cover that one up with something much better and get her initials somewhere else on my body because she's family and feels like my little sister. The reason I don't like this one is because my friend did it when he was drunk and it isn't good enough.

DAPPY AND TULISA'S TATT

TULISA

My tattoo on my shoulder I got when I was 16 and I wish I hadn't now. I'm scared of needles so I passed out when he did it. I looked on the internet and found the letters for my name in Ancient Greek and just put them in that order. Then I looked up the meaning of my name in Ancient Greek and it's Balance Between Good and Evil or an Equilibrium of Harmony. So to represent that I had the Ying Yang symbol put under my name and then I had my star sign Cancer underneath that.

But now I'm gonna get all three of them gone over with something better when I can think of it.

OOS

LEARN FROM THE MASTER

Dappy's dad Byron always wanted to be famous and helped us get together musically as 12-year-olds. He was in his own band as a youngster with his brother Steve – Tulisa's dad – and Tulisa's mum Anne, but it didn't happen for them.

They wanted to be rock stars – Byron even looked like Rod Stewart, and Steve looked like some kind of hunk back in the day, all big hair and denim like a heart-throb! They were 'the Greeks', and they did do well when they were in Mungo Jerry's band for a while. Their big tune was 'In the Summertime'.

Don't get me wrong, they didn't make a lot of money, but what they did make they used to build a small recording studio in Dollis Hill. During the day B worked six days a week as a barber to make ends meet and keep the studio running.

He would press up white labels for us, get us little write-ups in *DJ* magazine and always tell us, 'You lot are gonna make it. Everyone's gonna know about you, you'll be in all the papers.' And he believed it. He kept us motivated with that kind of encouragement from early on and made us all believe that we could be something else.

Basically, what B would do throughout the whole developing stages was he would always look out for us. He would get me and Dappy a Christmas present like a pair of speakers for the studio, then set up a PC for us, then maybe give us an old keyboard he had sitting in the back of the house and maybe an old mic from somewhere, so that we could make our own little set-up just for us.

We would spend days and nights on that equipment, and Tulisa's dad would come in as well and we learned how to use it all. We did loads of songs in there, just me and Dappy with help from B.

We got up to all sorts in there, but he always told us he would rather we did it there in front of him in the studio than out on the street and getting in trouble. He made us feel safe and it was comfortable to be around him so we wanted to go there. B let us get away with the small things and in return we listened to him about the big things.

And it was the same with Tulisa too. She used to be just as bad as us. She would be on the road, hanging around with all the same guys that we were, seeing the same kind of things. Tulisa would fight with the guys for hours, out there on the grass tussling and everything!

But slowly, bit by bit, we would spend more and more time in the studio and less and less time out messing about or getting into trouble. From about 14 to 18 the balance of my life moved away from street life and into studio and music life.

I think the reason B was so supportive and nurturing of us was because he had always wanted to make it himself, but he never really scaled the heights. But when he saw something in us he thought that we could live the dream that he never got to enjoy. So he channelled that energy into us lot.

He taught me life lessons away from the music side too. Everything that he ever told me makes sense to me now that he's gone. I never used to understand some of the mad talk he used to come out with.

He used to say, 'The vampires are gonna suck your blood, Fazer. They're gonna come and get you.' But I know what he meant now. He was talking about the leeches. The hangers-on that try to suck me dry – he showed me how to recognise those people. That's knowledge that I use in all aspects of my life – the ability to spot the users.

He was always telling us to be our own person, be individual and proud of it, work for your dreams. The main part of my personal philosophy and the N-Dubz philosophy comes from him, no two ways about it. And now, as we're a bit older and in a position to do so, we try and pass that knowledge on and take people under our wing too.

There's a youngster from my area called Fearless and he was going down the wrong path. He got into trouble with someone in a different area and it was all looking bad for him but now he's my boy. We bring him to the studio, make records with him, give him beats for no charge and try and encourage him. He's a good MC and better than most others out there and we make him channel his talent towards success not failure. And that's as a direct result of B's attitude and what he did for us. He was always like 'Bring all the ghetto boys here, bring them in here off the streets, man.'

He was almost like a community leader in a way. He'd walk into his own room and there'd be a big crew of youths in there that would intimidate a lot of people, but not him. He'd just bowl in and start talking with no hesitation. Once he brought in bags of fried chicken and chips from KFC. Everyone respected him. He was just one of those guys that no one would take the piss with.

The main thing was he WOULD NOT ALLOW negativity from anyone. He would not have it. If anyone tried to take us away from that dream of success as musicians, he would just stamp that out.

And he didn't let us get away with anything either. If I was supposed to be somewhere or meet someone and it was important, he would be around at my house early doors ringing on my doorbell to make sure I got up and kept my appointments. Say I was at some girl's house – he would track me down to whatever area I was in and make me go to the studio even if I just wanted to chill.

Our lives basically became set in three places: the studio, Uncle Steve's house with B, home to chill. Day in, day out. He just kept us at it. He made us believe that there was a way out at the same time as physically keeping us from being on the streets up to no good all the time.

He put us on a Crimestoppers tour at the age of 14 years old – when we all hated the police! We were going up and down the country doing gigs associated with the police in front of people that had never heard of us.

At the end of the night he'd give us our £200 we had earned and it felt good.

Dappy started at my school when we were 11 or 12 and Byron had a meeting with the headteacher. The head told him there was one person in the whole school that Dappy shouldn't be friends with. And that was me.

But I was the only person in that school that Dappy even slightly knew – of course we were gonna be tight.

So the day after that, I went back to Dappy's house to meet his mum and dad. As soon as she heard my name she said 'Oh my f'ing gosh!' and her whole face just looked unhappy. She called Byron in and started speaking to him in Greek and waving her arms about.

Byron said to me 'They told me not to let my son hang around with you, but I won't stop him. Don't you get my son into no shit though.'

And here's the funny part – the first time I met Byron, I stole his phone! I can't believe that even now! I was in the house after that and I saw the phone on the side when he left the room and I just pocketed it.

He came in and was cursing: 'Where's my f'ing phone? You – you little @*$! ... where's my f'ing phone?!' He pulled another phone out of his pocket and dialled a number and obviously his phone started ringing in my pocket. I made some rubbish excuse about using it and taking it by accident, but he wasn't having any of it.

He said, 'Don't lie to me, you wanted my phone. Okay – have it. I don't need it. I've got another one here, see? If you can't get your own then I will give it you if that's the only way.'

I didn't take it, but from then on I never took the piss with him
ever again. He showed me he wasn't a man to mess about with.
I was young and dumb, but I learned from him. And that was how
my relationship with B really started. He would always tell people
that story of how we met from then on.

I love that guy. He just got me and we had so many laughs together.

**Each month he would make up packages of pictures and
magazine cuttings and our latest tunes which he would send
to record companies and radio stations and the like. Hundreds
every month. We just had so many broken promises and people
wasting our time despite his hard work. People coming in saying
'I can make you the next big thing' or whatever – then nothing.**

It got to the point where B and us three got so sick of all of
that shit that we just took it into our own hands. B came to
us one day in 2006 and said, 'I'm not doing this package
shit no more. I'm sick of paper cuts and broken nails –
there's a new way, we are going to do it ourselves.'

He had found a young media student from Bournemouth
University called George Burt who wanted to make a video for us.
We met up and went for it. He did us a video for a tune called 'Every
Day of My Life' with one little JVC camera for £500! To do tracking
shots he just stuck it on a car and reversed it up the road while we
walked towards him. Let me put that in perspective. The video we
just shot with Mr Hudson for 'Playing with Fire' cost £45,000!

'Every Day of My Life' got on the night-time playlist for Channel U – not even daytime so hardly anyone saw it. After that happened I had a proper little wobble when I thought that it might just not happen for us. The dream could be over.

But B wouldn't allow any of us to think like that. You can't just lie down after a fall and not get up, he said, so we tried again – we spent £1,000 with the same guy doing a video for 'Better Not Waste My Time'. We rented a better camera this time around and, funnily enough, this time we got on the daytime playlist on Channel U so people had a chance to actually see it. And there was a good response. People liked the catchiness of it and started clocking on to us a little bit.

I remember we went and did a show in Liverpool and people were just there because they'd seen the video. They didn't even really know the lyrics but they wanted to see what we were all about – but only 70 people in a 2,000 capacity venue! It was depressing times because we had felt that we were starting to build momentum. I only remembered that the other day when my friend gave me a picture he had taken from the back of the stage of us lot in front of 16,000 people at a sold-out Manchester Arena.

But then people started voting for the video on Channel U – they wanted to see it more because we had a proper hook and singing choruses that they could sing along with. We were at No. 1 on there for something mad like 16 weeks in summer 2006. That was the time the buzz around us first started to develop, even though it was only on an underground TV station.

Sometimes I'd be walking down the road and I'd see someone do a little double take, or one brave person would say, 'Are you that guy from that group that are on Channel U?' They didn't even know what we were called!

So now we were starting to make it and it was all off our own backs. Us three and B had done it because none of the labels would touch us.

Until then. They couldn't ignore all that success on Channel U and so Polydor came to us and offered us a little single deal. They gave us £25,000 and told us to get on with it. Like give the mice a little bit of cheese and see what they do with it. We had to manufacture the single, distribute it, promote it and do the video ourselves out of that money.

We wanted to strike while the iron was still hot from Channel U and we made 'I Swear'. We used the same guy again – George Burt – and spent £3,000 of that money on a proper HD camera, £2,000 on lighting and £1,000 on someone B knew to do promotion and all that.

It left us with £19,000. And that's where B came in again and used his wisdom. He told us to use that money to make a landing mat for ourselves so that even if everything failed, we'd still be all right. So we spent all that money on the studio, buying top-of-the-range mics and gear. And that meant we could just make record after record after record because we had EVERYTHING we needed to produce hit tunes now. Plus we had our camera and lights, so we started working like troupers. We did 'Feva Las Vegas', 'Love For My Slum', 'Ouch' – all ready to come out … so many tunes!

This is all while the world was going mad for Simon Cowell and reality TV music shows – and there's us doing it all for ourselves.

> The first show we did after 'I Swear' came out was crazy. It was in Camberley of all places. We walked out on stage and people were screaming for us. It was difficult to take in. I wasn't ready for that day. I got pulled off the stage and Dappy had to jump into the crowd to try and help get me back out again.

I looked over at B by the side of the stage and I could see in his face how happy he was. We were living his dream as well as ours. That was one of the best moments of my life – when we got off the stage, I'd never seen anything like the look on his face before. He was so happy and telling us we were stars and gonna be famous.

Two days later he died. That was in April 2007.

> He never tried to claim credit at all. He always told people, 'These guys are going to be superstars. I don't produce music – they do it all by themselves.' But we could never have done it without him. We would have fallen off long before we got anywhere.

B was our saviour. He was the one who made us believe we could become what we are right now and then take it to a worldwide level. Usually people pray to God, but we don't. Us three pray to B to guide us. I still have dreams about him, but that stuff is just too personal to share with anyone.

> That's why after we won our first Mobo award – for Best Newcomer in 2007 – we dedicated it to B. He'd only just died a few months previously and it was down to him that we had been able to win that award. We felt that win was recognition for his belief and for him.

When I think about B dying, I still get mad. It kills me to even think about it. The day before he died I was with him because we had to talk about moving into new studios as the contract was running out on our old place. He convinced me about somewhere he had found, and we went our separate ways after agreeing to talk about it later. He called that night and asked me to come round, but I was off in another part of town and didn't make it.

I met Dappy the next day and he was screwing because he'd come back from football the night before and was locked out of his house. He had to sleep over at a friend's house. We spent the day in town and got mobbed at McDonald's in Marble Arch – the whole place came to a standstill and we were on a high.

We headed back to Camden, only to find Dappy's mum standing outside their house with all her suitcases – she had just come back from Greece. She was fuming because she couldn't get in either and B hadn't picked her up from the airport.

We were knocking on the door a lot but we noticed that B's van was still parked up outside. He used to have a habit of going for long walks by the canal on his own just to clear his head, so we guessed that he must be doing that.

But after a while he still wasn't back and then we spotted his keys and his phone through the window on the table. Dappy was sitting downstairs talking to people, so I got a clothes hanger from the neighbours and managed to hook the keys out so I could open the door.

As soon as I opened the door I could feel a vibe that something was wrong. I didn't want to walk in there first or let Dappy's mum go in, so one of our friends walked ahead of me.

We looked in different rooms but when I walked into the living-room I saw him sitting on the sofa with his hands behind his head. And I just knew he was dead straight away.

He had died in front of the TV. I looked at the screen and it was on Channel U. He had died sitting there on his own looking for our video.

I tried not to let Dappy's mum come in and see him, but I couldn't stop her. I thought she would break down when she saw him, but I've never seen someone act like she did. She started trying to tidy up the flat and asking me to help, and she was shaking badly.

Dappy didn't even want to come in. As soon as I walked out and he saw my face he knew. He came up in the end when we laid B down on the couch and put a blanket over him and he just looked defeated. Then he walked out again with his head hanging.

We had a show the next day and we weren't gonna do it, but I got everyone up. I told them he had died waiting to see our video, we can't not do this, we HAVE to do this for him.

It was the hardest show of our lives. We were crying on the stage and everything.

After that things just became a whirlwind. We hardly even had time to grieve because our careers were taking off so fast. Like I said in 'Papa', it's like he sacrificed his life for the love of success. Like in order for us to be successful, he died. That's how it feels to me.

He died from a heart attack and I knew he was ill. He'd been saying some weird stuff before he died, and we'd been having arguments with him. I would see him at night and he'd be coughing a lot and being sick. I think he knew something was wrong because he kept saying things like 'One day you guys will be here on your own and I won't be here to look after you.' He was laughing and saying, 'You guys don't like me now but don't worry, I won't be here forever.'

We got closer than ever after his death. And we needed that because people tried it on with us. We sold something like 42,000 copies of 'I Swear' and we didn't see a penny from it. That would have never happened to us if B had been around. It just showed us.

We knew from then we had to take what B had taught us and use it. It was like the final stage of us growing up. We had to take our business under our control and make it work for us properly. We employed accountants, lawyers and management between the three of us to make sure we could never get stiffed again.

We're our own bosses now. It's all down to us. The Christmas 2009 tour we did, we worked out the budget on that. We wanted to make some money for the festive season. We outlayed £100,000 to do the tour – and tripled that money. That's business.

TULISA'S DUBPLATE DRAMA

Dubplate Drama is a TV series that started when I was 17 and I used to love it.

MC Shystie is the main star of the programme and it's about a female MC called Dionne and other young kids involved in music.

It was on Channel 4 and it was the best thing I had ever seen. It was about me and my mates pretty much. I remember one night sitting in my living-room wishing I could be on it and thinking about what character I would play on the show.

When they came to make the second series of it in 2007,

they approached me for a part and gave Dappy and Fazer little cameos. I couldn't believe it — it was sick! I went there for the role of a slutty chick, but I didn't want to play her and after my audition they said they wanted me to play a more emotional character anyway.

So they gave me the role of Laurissa — the babymother of a guy called Bones who was one of Dionne's rivals. It was quite a small role, but I did have to play a really emotional scene when he got killed. So for my first bit of acting I had to conjure up some really big emotions. I loved it even though it was a challenge.

They were really pleased with me and said they wished they'd given my character a bigger part to play because they were so happy with me. Guess what — series three came and they wrote me a proper big part. I became one of the main characters, Dionne's arch-rival.

I also get with a character called Prangers who's played by Ricci Hartnett, a professional actor who's starred in films like *Rise of the Footsoldier* and *28 Days Later*. I had to play his young girlfriend and be into cocaine and other drugs, so it was a very serious role. There were scenes when my boyfriend was very abusive and scenes when I had to sniff up baby food off toilet seats as if it was cocaine — it was hard work!

Ricci is such a great guy, he's definitely a friend for life. I learned a lot from him about acting. It was so funny because his character is this evil guy who swears and abuses me and I'd be screaming back at him until they said 'cut' and we'd fall about in hysterics.

It was good times then because *Uncle B* had gone platinum and we were about to go on tour which was a sell-out.

I had to cram all my filming into two weeks before the tour and I was rehearsing for the tour at the same time too, so I was exhausted. The boys complained about being tired at rehearsals, and I was the one that when rehearsals finished, would have to go and work until 4 a.m. filming. I was knackered.

They're talking about bringing out *Dubplate Drama The Movie*, which I'm also involved in, and that's gonna be amazing. It probably won't happen for another two years, but I'm co-writing part of the script for my character — and I've just come up with a genius idea for my character.

MY LOVELY UNCLE

Uncle B always made us believe that we could do it, but at the same time he always pushed us too. He was a very harsh man in that he didn't believe in self-pity. He had no time for it. If we were feeling down he always used to tell us to stop moping around and get on with it.

I used to have arguments with him when I was having a really tough time with the bullies, and even then he would say some really harsh stuff to me. He would always say, 'Just because this has happened to you, you think you're worse off than other people. There's people dying in this world. Get up off your arse and do something.' Sometimes I would hate him for it. I didn't understand how he could say that to me when I was going through such a horrible time.

Through all of my year out of school time as a 14-year-old I was obviously doing my music as well. The studio became another escape route for me – struggling in there after I'd had a kicking or something. Every time I'd get beaten up, I'd go to the studio and record.

I remember turning up once with bust lips and black eyes, crying to the boys, and them saying let's write a song. Let's channel it into music. We did that a lot, and my music was my saviour. It was the thing that let me know it was all gonna be all right. I would sit there cursing all those girls' names and telling myself that at least I had a talent and that they would end up nowhere, even though now I don't blame them anymore. I thank B for giving me that opportunity – even if sometimes he made me cry too.

> **Once when my mum was really ill he said, 'All that shit at home that's doing your nut in – why are you bringing it into the studio to do our nut in?' I really did hate him for some of the things he said, but looking back on it he gave me what I needed. I did need strong words to make me fight back and not give in. I was in that depression mode, feeling sorry for myself, and it was being fed to some extent by my own self-pity.**

I remember one day he was driving me home from the studio and I was at a really low point. I had lost motivation and wasn't putting in any effort with my singing. He told me: 'Some people are depressives and some people aren't. You need to accept that you are a depressed person. Don't try and fight it. Accept it, deal with it, live with it and get on with it. Just embrace your depression and learn how to live with it and not let it hold you back.' It was proper tough love he gave me.

We would gets calls from labels all the time. We would meet up with them left, right and centre and get let down all the time. It became a regular thing and we would just end up sitting in some office waiting for them to feed us another load of rubbish. It was nothing but setbacks and knockbacks and it started to look like it was never gonna happen for us.

Again, it was B who held us together. There was no option of quitting with him. He took the pressure off our shoulders because the option of giving up was removed from the equation.

Plus he used to withhold some of the negative stuff and only feed us positives. He'd even make things up to keep our heads up and give us hope. Sometimes it was complete bollocks! But it worked!

We had huge arguments in the time before he passed and we spent a long time barely talking. Eventually he called me and said, 'Forget the music for a second, I just want to be your uncle again. Before all this you were just my little niece and I want that back. No matter what happens, remember I am your uncle and I love you.'

It was about a week later that he passed away. That was the last conversation I had with him.

Sometimes I did doubt him despite all the belief he showed in us, but I honestly think he was psychic or something. He knew his fate and he knew that he was meant to help us on this journey. He felt – in the same way that I felt it as a kid – that this was just meant to be.

I remember sitting on my grandparents' roof out in Greece as a child and him teaching me karate. He was a real preacher and used to believe in all the martial-arts teachings and about cleansing the soul, positive and negative energy and that kind of thing. He used to call all the negative people vampires. Even though I'm very religious, the things he taught me still make up a huge part of my belief and spirituality.

I was filming for my first little appearance in *Dubplate Drama* in 2007 when I found out that B had died. I had just filmed a scene where I had to cry my eyes out because I had lost someone close to me. To get into character I'd been trying to imagine losing someone close to me, because it had never actually happened to me in real life.

I turned my phone on and a load of texts came through from Dappy and Fazer saying they needed to speak to me. I started panicking about something being wrong, and the cast and crew were trying to calm me down as I called Dappy.

He refused to tell me over the phone and drove with Fazer to where we were filming. All this time I was phoning all my family to see what was going on, but I couldn't get through to anyone. For some reason I had a sense someone had died.

They turned up and Dappy told me to sit down because he had some seriously bad news for me. But I was getting angry and shouting at them to tell me what was wrong.

Dappy said, 'Are you ready for this … B's dead.'

He said it that simply. He told me how it happened and how they found him.

For a couple of seconds I felt my heart rate go up and I thought I was going to have a heart attack because the news was too much for me to physically take. Then I blacked out and I can remember a few people holding me as I fell.

When I woke up the tears came flooding out and this loud wailing noise came out of me in front of everyone. I couldn't stop it. They took me out on to a patch of grass outside and I kept crying hysterically. Then it struck me: however bad I was feeling, it was Dappy's dad, so I just looked at his face and saw his distress and it made it even worse to think of what he was going through. I grabbed him and hugged him and I remember that he wasn't able to cry. He was numb. He couldn't deal with the emotion and I just kept saying how sorry I was.

Someone drove me home with him and he said he just wanted to come to my house and sit there. We sat in the back of this convertible with the roof off, and there was this beautiful sunset and a cool breeze. Neither of us spoke for half an hour and we just watched the sunset as we squeezed each other's hands so tight it hurt.

Uncle B was everything to us. There would be no N-Dubz without him. All the stress and pressure that came from getting us to where we were pretty much killed him, so he died for our success. He was such an inspiring person with so much

passion and belief. It wasn't just with us either – he was the same with any little ghetto kid he could help. He would bring them into the studio and try and get them to do positive things. He was like a ghetto Mother Teresa and a wonderful person to be around that should be remembered and looked up to. I love him very much and miss him to this day.

Winning the Mobo Best Newcomers in 2007 meant everything to us. Dappy was wearing his sunglasses even though it was night-time because it meant so much to him. His dad wasn't long gone and we were there as a result of that man's belief. Dappy wanted to win that award so badly for his dad that he couldn't bear the thought of not getting it. He had wet eyes from the emotions running through him all day, just hoping that we would win it for B, so I told him to keep his shades on. Imagine if we hadn't won and the camera cut to his face and he had tears in his eyes. It wouldn't have been a good look!

We were up against Mutya and I was convinced we weren't gonna win – and then I heard them say 'N-Dubz'.
It was unreal to me.

Before I could even get out of my seat, Dappy was half-way to the stage looking like he was flying. That was definitely a lift that we needed and I remember feeling very emotional up on stage. It meant everything for Uncle B. We just felt like he was sitting there at the table smiling at us.

PAPA

My dad was a bass player in Mungo Jerry and with the money from that he built himself a little studio in Dollis Hill called Jumbo Studios. Everyone around that area of London knows that place. It's about two feet away from the tube station. I spent so much time there.

From as far back as I can remember my dad was involved in music, doing music, talking about music. From being a tiny little kid I'd be messing about with guitars or fiddling with instruments or whatever.

When we were living in the little shoebox in Camden – me, my mum and dad and my older brother – my dad gave me a four-track recording device and a crappy little microphone, which are the first pieces of kit lots of musicians start with. I was aged about nine and he would always encourage me with the music. He would tell me that I was gonna be a rapper and a singer – you're gonna be a star, he said. He made me believe that it was my destiny.

He and Tulisa's dad Steve taught me everything I know about how to make music. That's how I learned that you have to use real guitarists and violinists to get a proper rich sound – not by using the synth sounds.

My dad was a big man in the community and everyone loved
him. All my friends looked up to him and called him Uncle B.
Even I would call him that. I never used to call my dad 'Dad'.
Never. He was always just B to me. I've only started calling
him Dad since he died.

Sadly, thoughts of my dad are starting to slide away a bit now
because it's been three years and I'm starting to forget, but all I need
to see is one little picture, or hear his voice for a second and it all
comes flooding back to me and I get depressed for about two weeks.

He didn't ever want any harm to come to anyone. That just
wasn't in him. Sometimes I would doubt him. He would find me
with drugs or maybe some sort of weapon and shout at me,
'What are you doing with this in your hand? You don't need that,
you are going to go down, YOU ARE GOING TO GO DOWN.'

And to this day I will tell you knives are a bad thing. If you wanna
make something out of your life, don't carry a knife. And if someone
comes to try and rob you with a knife, you should run for your life.
Don't play the hero – it's not worth it.

I thanked my dad for opening my eyes in 'Papa Can You Hear Me?'. He
told me I didn't need those kind of tools to get by in life. At the time I was
so angry. I couldn't see any other way to make money or get by. The next
day I went to him all pissed off and asked him what I was supposed to do.

He said, 'Don't worry, it's not over yet, I've got something for
you', then drove me to the studio in his old green van. I walked
in and there it was. He had bought me a new microphone – a
Neumann U87. That's pretty much the best studio mic you can
have and that's when our vocals started sounding proper and
our material began to sound professional for the first time.

He was a smart guy. He took away the badness and showed me the direction to go in very subtly. I was about 16 or 17 then, and that's the time we started writing our first album, *Uncle B*. A few years down the line that album named after him has sold half a million copies.

Sometimes I must admit he would get a little bit too carried away with his ideas and say some very funny things. He'd say 'In the video, you should have some guitar players dressed in ninja suits and everyone else dressed in black. Me and your Uncle Stevie will do it. We will make the part work for you!'

We used to crack up and say to him there's no way you're coming in our video. Then he'd laugh and start telling us, 'You're nothing, man, you're amateur to us, you little rascals. Shut up, Dappy, you're my sperm – you be quiet!'

He knew N-Dubz were a very unique thing from the moment we first got together. He just knew, and that's why he had such belief in us and refused to let negative people be around us and our music.

I remember one time when I was still proper young and I went into the studio and this guy who had a couple of tunes out was in there too. He said to me, 'Why are you spittin' at 150 miles an hour? That's no good.'

I was a bit baffled to be honest because this older man was being all negative when I was trying to spit.

My dad came in and started telling him we were good and we were just play-listed on Kiss FM.

The guy checked on the Kiss playlist right then and said, 'Nope, you're nowhere to be found, little man. My record's at No. 19 but you're not there at all.'

My dad was trying to speak to the guy without us hearing but we could hear him whispering, 'Shh, I'm just trying to make them feel a bit good about themselves.' Later, as we left the studio, I overheard my dad telling him he was a wanker.

Boom! A couple of years down the line and we're doing a sold-out show at the O2 Arena in London and I see this guy standing outside waiting to get in. I brought him in all friendly like and reminded him of the time he told me I was crap. I properly enjoyed making him feel stupid in front of people at MY show after he'd told me I couldn't do anything in front of my dad.

I'll never forget the day my dad died. I had been out all day and I got home around midnight, but I couldn't get in. My mum was in Greece and I didn't have my key so I was banging on the door for my dad to let me in. No answer at all.

I looked through the letter box and my mum's puppy Lily was looking at me and then looking over her shoulder at the living-room all funny.

I could see the living-room light was on. But of course there was no one in there I thought. Next up I called his phone and I could hear it ringing just inside the front door. I was screwing at him for leaving his phone. Then I went to check for his green van outside, wishing it wouldn't be there because that would be odd.

It was there still. All I could do was go downstairs to my mate's house and stay the night down there in his room.

The next day there was still no answer at my door, the dog's still there and everything. I had no idea what was going on so I went and met up with Fazer and a few other people and just thought to sit it out until my dad got home. By the time we came back to mine, my mum was standing outside with all her suitcases and my brother.

DAPPY

I knew what time it was then, even though everyone else just thought B had gone out or something. I was sitting downstairs in the square and I knew something was up – I knew it inside me.

The minute they got the door open I was shouting up at them to not let my mum go in first. I knew someone was going to go in to the living-room and then come out in hysterics and I didn't want that to be my mum.

Fazer came out a minute later and I thought I heard him say 'It's cool' so I jumped up all happy and relieved like 'Yes!' But then I looked properly and I could see he was rubbing his head looking all mad. Then my brother came out too and I knew.

> I ran upstairs and saw my dad on the couch. I touched his head and put my lips on his lips trying to put air in his lungs and everything.

I went out in to the hallway but I couldn't help keep looking in the little mirror and seeing my dad's feet in the reflection – that was all I could see. And I was crying and crying and crying.

> I went back outside and watched the ambulance arrive and the men bring him out of our house in a black bag and drive him away.

> Fazer and me went to tell T and *Dubplate Drama* and … then was the funeral. I try not to think about it now because it still gets me down to this day and it's hard.

Before he died he kept telling me that it was going to be different soon. I think he knew that he was ill and had a very big problem inside his heart and his lungs.

He kept saying 'You know where I want you to take this' over and again – and I DID know. If only I could tell him now that we sell out tours and have two massive albums, three Mobo awards and a No. 1 single.

This is where he wanted us to be.

PART 3
PUSHING ON AFTER BYRON

STAYING HUMBLE

After the success of 'I Swear', Polydor wanted to take us on further and re-release 'Better Not Waste My Time', so they gave us another single deal with an option for an album. It went Top 20, which was a result bearing in mind we had already released it before and loads of people had bought it already. We had our loyal fans to thank again.

So after that we took Polydor every one of our songs, from 'Papa' to 'Ouch' – and they didn't want them. They said they couldn't even see a chorus on 'Ouch'! We took them a lot of massive records and they couldn't even see what they had in front of them.

But it got worse, because they tried to push us in a different direction and take us away from what we knew to be good. They tried to bring writers in with us and change up our thing that we had built from scratch. Now you have to keep an open mind about things, but we went into one session and knew that it wasn't right for us to be doing that. It wasn't being honest to ourselves. We spent a day with a producer and a songwriter and thought 'What the hell are we doing this for?'

In 2008 we finally just asked Polydor to please let us go and do our own thing because they were making us come to a standstill. All the buzz had started dying down around us because they did not have the vision that we had.

So we took it back to where we had came from. We got our uni boy George again, paid up and made the video for 'Ouch' ourselves. We just called up all our old connections, told them were going back to the drawing board and everyone was there but B. We were doing it for B.

We put it out on YouTube and MTV Base played it too.
We got nine million hits on YouTube in one month.

Guess what – Polydor came back to us and asked how we would feel about releasing 'Ouch' with them. I asked our new manager to kindly, in the most professional way possible, tell them to go and shove their offer up their arse.

It was the right move because our current label – All Around The World – got in touch and we released 'Ouch' as a physical and digital single through them. They had the same vision as us and continued to set things up so we could release 'Papa' as a follow-up single. They threw £30,000 at us to do the 'Papa' video because they believed in us and then more for 'Strong Again' after that. That was the start of a beautiful relationship. I wouldn't want to be with any other record label than them now. This small independent label is doing a better job than any major I know.

We have 100 per cent control of everything we do both creatively and monetarily. If they want to spend £50,000 on TV marketing for an *X Factor* advert, we might tell them to spend £30,000 on that and the other £20,000 on billboards. And they HAVE to do it. If we don't side for it, it can't happen. We have earned the right to have that sort of control. And it's an equal split between the three of us. All power and money is split 33.3 per cent each. Our company is N-Dubz Music LLP – we registered at Companies House in London!

If I sit back and look at that – considering where I came from – I have to say I am proud of that achievement. To be one of three bosses of this thing. Sometimes I still have to pinch myself to believe I have made it. That's why, when we won two Mobos in 2009, it meant a lot. Especially winning Best Album for *Uncle B*. It meant the world because we'd done so much work on it.

We're not some major-label act with 15 people working on our album to make it win – it's just us in our little shack of a studio. We put our hearts, soul, sweat and blood into that. Those songs are like our kids, so it's emotional to us. Best Album was what we wanted the most, and getting Best UK Act was just a bonus – the icing on the cake.

This is my job now. It's not just some fun with music – I have to take it seriously day in day out.

I can still remember the first time I was out on the street and a complete stranger recognised me. I was going to the shop to get some eggs for my mum and there was a bunch of schoolkids in the shop who mobbed me. They were screaming and everything and I didn't know how to react. I was just a bit dazed. They were asking to have pictures with me and when I asked what for, they were like 'Because you're famous, you're on TV in that band.'

I've learned how to deal with that now. I know I'm famous and I slightly feel like I am too. I'll go out with two hoodies on and a baseball cap and people will still clock me and I hear them going 'Blah blah blah … N-Dubz!' I had to get escorted out of Westfield Shopping Centre once because it got too much.

If it wasn't for the fans we wouldn't be where we are right now, full stop. If we didn't have people who believe in our music and went out and bought it, we'd get dropped by record labels and we'd have nothing. That's why we're so thankful to all you people who bought our music. You are Number One to us.

When I go to shows and hear people screaming for N-Dubz I'm still like 'Why are you screaming for me?' I just want to climb into the crowd and give you lot a group hug because you changed my whole life for me. I never forget that, because once you do, that's when you start flying and you lose yourself.

I always have time for the fans. If I get stopped on the street and get mobbed by 20 or 30 people, I will take pictures with every single one of them. I talk to them, I stay humble. If I'm on my way to Starbucks and someone comes up to me I'll invite them for a coffee and a chat. I don't know you but you bought my CD, so I've got time for you.

I know Dappy and T feel the same. That's the thing with N-Dubz – we're like the Spice Girls! Everyone's got their favourite Spice and everyone's got their favourite member from N-Dubz.

I interact with fans online all the time. It's properly important to me. I run the MySpace, the Bebo, the Facebook and the Twitter from my home still. When people go on there and talk to me, it really is me they are talking to. I have to keep people involved and let them feel they are a part of the movement.

TULISA'S GUIDE TO FASHION & STYLE

I'm like the most unfashionable person in the world! I NEVER dress like I do on stage in real life, it's just too much effort and hassle to do all that work every day.

Just do 'you' is my best advice.

Don't follow too many trends if you can help it.

For me, I'm either slobbing about or going out, so I have two extremes. On a lazy day I normally wear leggings, Ugg boots and long T-shirts. Maybe a thick hoody if it's cold. Or maybe Adidas trainers and a velour tracksuit with my hair scraped back and no make-up on at all.

If I'm going out, I always use my spotstick to cover any little blemishes I might have and then a bit under my eyes to cover any bags, plus a bit of mascara and that's it. I don't like to cake it on.

If I'm going clubbing then I'm a bit of a cliché. I'm a bit of a Barbie

doll so I like really girly stuff. My idea of a decent outfit would be some killer heels, a nice pair of leggings and a sexy corset or a cute girly dress with my hair all done up nicely. I love pink.

I never go too heavy on the eye make-up because I don't like that drag queen look.

In terms of foundation, I keep that to a minimum too. Just concealer, blusher and powder.

When you're dressing to impress, you don't want to overdo it and be too sexy.

I would never do legs, belly and cleavage. That's just way too much. I'd show a bit of cleavage and some leg, but never all three.

I believe in looking classy 100 per cent.

I don't really buy anything that costs over 50 quid, except maybe trainers. Any designer stuff I've got has been given to me. If I go shopping I normally go to Brent Cross, Kilburn High Road or Camden High Street for the market stalls. I refuse to be extorted.

Don't be fooled into thinking you have to spend big bucks to look good.

LOW DAT LABEL

After the success of 'You Better Not Waste My Time' Polydor came with a single deal and we used a little money from them to bring out 'I Swear', which took us up to yet another level again because Kiss FM started playing it. That's why I always give shouts out to Jez Welham, because he was the first major DJ to show belief and back us on radio.

But even then there were some major knockbacks and setbacks. Polydor didn't release anything with us after that. We kept making tunes and releasing stuff on Channel U but the label didn't help us at all. They just didn't understand us, didn't think we would work commercially and didn't believe in us, even though we'd won our Mobo.

We were 100 per cent confident in the music that we were making and I personally thought everyone at that label was completely mad for not seeing what they had in front of them. All they could think of doing was re-releasing 'Better Not Waste My Time', which we didn't want them to do as everyone already had it.

Our fans wanted new material from us but Polydor weren't getting it. We took them all our big songs and they didn't like any of them so they tried to push us in a different direction. They put us in a studio once with a George Michael producer and someone who had written with Leona Lewis – and it wasn't us. If they wanted that, they should have just taken any three kids off the street and made a new pop band.

I would never have sold out like that. Even if they'd given us a cheque for £250,000. Because then what? That would have been the last music payment I ever got because you can't make music that isn't true to you. People will see through it.

> They said they wanted to make us appeal to a wider market, but we knew 30-year-olds would never be our main market. That wasn't who we were aiming at. The kids like us were our market, so we wanted to keep making music for them and not try to please people who were never gonna like our sound.

The reality hit me when we stopped at a service station on the way to a gig and a girl said to us, 'I remember you! You're those three kids that had that song ages ago.' So we had to leave Polydor before our careers were ruined.

If we hadn't left Polydor then it would have been complete career suicide for us. It was a bold move for us to part ways, but we KNEW our music would sell and we had belief in it – we just needed to find a label that could see our vision as well.

> That's when we did 'Ouch' ourselves in a mate's big house and just had another crack at going it alone. It went huge on Channel U and MTV Base and the fans loved it. We got millions of hits.

Off the back of that All Around The World Records got in touch with us and we signed up with them in 2008. They had the belief in us that we had always been looking for and they took us on to release 'Papa' and 'Strong Again' and then our debut album *Uncle B* which went platinum and then some, selling 500,000 copies!

By then there was no doubting that these kids sold records! Every label that didn't believe in us and chose not to sign us must be kicking themselves now. Everyone at Polydor who had been slagging us off and saying we were shit must feel stupid. We had the last laugh.

We had great support from Jonathan Shalit at ROAR Global as well. He was interested in managing us when Uncle B was still around, but B wasn't having any of it at the time. But he was having a change of mind just a few days before he died because doing everything for us was starting to tire him out.

He was saying he needed someone to take over looking after us. So when he died, we looked at Jonathan and ROAR Global and saw that he worked with big-name players. For us that was important and he looked impressive so we signed up and haven't looked back.

OUR TING DIS

Musically, after my dad died it was like it reinforced us as a group and made us stronger than ever. We became the best we had ever been. Every time we would go in the studio we were so focused and determined to make sure we got to where B wanted us to be.

On a personal level I still find it hard without my dad around. When I get upset or angry and want someone to talk to, he's not there any more. He was my best friend. I would tell him anything and he would always have good advice for me.

The video that we made with George Burt was when the buzz first started happening for us. George Burt is my family. He's my guy. If he needs a place to stay, money – anything – I will give him it no questions asked. My dad found him and introduced him to me when George was still at university. He wanted to make videos for us and he was up for doing it on the proper cheap.

When he first came to meet us in Camden in 2006 before anyone knew who we were he was the poshest boy I'd ever met. I toughened him up quickly, telling him how to hold himself and carry himself on the street. He was shitting himself that night when we were filming 'Every Day of My Life' round that way. Some crackhead was eyeing up his camera and there was all ghetto yoots everywhere – he was nervy! Now – he's one of us! He's not scared of no one and nothing.

Anyway, we did that little video and it didn't even really get noticed, but we did a follow-up together for 'Better Not Waste My Time'. We spent a lot of time on it doing the fades and making it look proper good. We directed, edited, styled and did everything for that video ourselves. It went to No. 1 on Channel U for untold amounts of weeks and that was it – N-Dubz had arrived.

That's when I started getting recognised. I used to wake up and think to myself, 'I'm going out today to see how many people recognise me.' I'd put on the same clothes and hat that I had in the video and go out my house. If someone asked if I was Dappy I'd say 'Yeah, man, what you sayin? NaNaNiiiii!'

Whatever person says they never went out and looked for their fame when it first started is a liar, I tell you that much for free right now. Of course you wanna go and see if people know who you are.

Next up came 'I Swear', because Polydor had got interested in us after all the Channel U plays and gave us a £25,000 single deal sometime in 2007.

That's when we felt like we were on top of the world. Like we had finally made it.

You have to understand we had spent so many years knocking on record labels' doors with my dad and being told 'No'. The amount of times we heard that we were too young, or not ready yet, or didn't have enough saleability. The amount of times we'd heard my dad say, 'Don't worry, guys, we'll find another way, we'll go to another label.'

And then one day my dad came in and said, 'Guess what, guys – you got yourselves a record deal with Polydor.'

'I Swear' sent things mad for us. Doing shows, people singing our songs and N-Dublets starting to appear regularly at our events. Thing is though – we weren't really seeing eye to eye with the people at Polydor.

They were clueless and blind. Only one person had faith in us there – our A&R guy there called Ivan Deer, and he was as frustrated with it as us.

I told them we needed to release 'Ouch' as our next proper big single to take things up to another level. And all they kept saying was 'Where's the chorus?' So they made us re-release 'Better Not Waste My Time' – not the smartest move. Remember everyone's already got that tune and I was telling them we needed to come with something new for the fans.

The tune got in the Top 20 and I was very, very upset and pissed off because we would have blown up then and there if we'd released 'Ouch' instead. They just would not listen to what we were trying to tell them. Even after we won our first Mobo for Best Newcomer after my dad died they wouldn't pay any attention and there was a big gap where we didn't release anything at all. They properly stalled us.

So we started doing stuff on our own since they were just trying to shelve us. We made 'Love For My Slum' and 'Feva Las Vegas' and just kept some kind of vibe going on Channel U as best we could. We had a proper little following off the back of what we were doing and we had so much confidence that 'Ouch' was a hit that we decided to cancel it with Polydor.

We went on our own and made 'Ouch' into a video using George again and went old school on it. I remember the first time I saw it on TV for its first play in 2008 and it looked like a proper expensive video. Seven grand is all that cost. Seven grand and untold blood, sweat and tears making it work.

Two months later, when Polydor saw how many millions of hits that video got on YouTube, they came back to us begging to let them release it.

That video smashed up everything and went on all the channels. We told them to piss directly off. We won a Silver Cleff award for that song for the amount of hits it got on the internet.

After all that stalling from Polydor, we boosted right back up in popularity again with just that one tune. We were bigger even than when we did 'Better Not Waste My Time' and 'I Swear'.

That's when the offers came in to sign us up again. We looked at an offer from Warner Brothers and we didn't like it at all. The two guys that came to see us were looking after Ironik and Wiley at the time. They sat down with us and told us we had to be a finished and polished product like Ironik. All three of us looked at each other and started cracking up – proper pointing at them and laughing in their faces. Then I told them to leave my studio and went mad at them. Trying to tell me I have to be like Ironik. Someone who will never even be able to think about reaching the kind of sales we were capable of and have since achieved. Now I'm not cussing Ironik, he's a great young lad and got some good tunes, but we're looking to go worldwide and I don't see Ironik as that kind of artist.

Now I look back and still recall when I got my first pay-cheque from my publisher. We got £250,000 to split between me, Fazer and T. We got our Coutts bank cards that same day and I was dressed like a dirty little hoodrat still. That card was for an account which had £25,000 for each of us. I couldn't believe it. Me – with that kind of money? I splashed the lot. I didn't do anything sensible with it financially. Maybe a little chain is all I've got to show for it somewhere.

But what I did do is look after some people. I helped out my friends because that's the type of person I am. I know Fazer did the same thing with his money as well. I regret not spending the bit I kept back for myself on something more sensible than jewellery, but I have no regrets about looking out for my people I had grown up with. Friends and family are the most important assets you can have in life, so it's only right that if you've got, then you make sure they've got too. And I still look after people to this day.

I'm a people person and that's why we went with All Around The World as a record label and hooked up with Jonathan Shalit to manage us.

They have the same vision as us and we get full creative control. If we wanna release another album in three weeks' time, the label will listen to us and it will most probably happen.

Me and Fazer are the A&Rs. We choose the records that are gonna come out and decide on how we are gonna sound. No one else – it's our ting dis. And my dad was right to believe in us, like our label and management do now.

When we won Best UK Act and Best Album at the Mobo Awards in 2009 that was just a proper boost. We're the best band now, simple. That means everyone recognises it and it's indisputable. Boom – we have to carry on upwards now.

PART 4
N-DUBZ DOMINATION: TODAY AND TOMORROW

FAZER ON MUSIC AND THE N-DUBZ TECHNIQUE

I come from a musical background so I get a lot of my love of music from my parents. My mum's a drummer and my dad plays blues harmonica and my whole house is like a museum of music.

I love hip-hop but I always keep an open mind because that's how I keep our sound fresh. I still listen to Sting, Phil Collins, Queen and George Michael. In my car, my first set radio station is Magic FM. You listen to those old songs and you learn so much from the music and the way it was constructed. With so much care and craftsmanship. I listen to those tunes and I ask myself 'Why is it not like that anymore? Why do people keep it so unimaginative?'

And we use their old recipes. We take what they used to do and apply that to our music in our studio and that's why our songs are different from everyone else's. We constantly take the songs up higher and higher throughout each tune.

Neither Dappy or me are better than the other when it comes to spittin'. We're different from each other which adds to our unique sound. Dappy has come into his own as a lyricist AND a vocalist. Dappy's more of a singer vocalist than me, whereas I'm a straight MC, that's it.

Lyrically we're at the same level. We'll kill a bar each and we both make each other better. If he says a verse I don't like in the studio, I'll tell him and he'll work on it until it's better. He'll do the same with me.

There's a tune on the new album called 'Say It's Over' and the first verse I wrote for it and recorded — Dappy didn't like it. He just looked at me and said, 'Fazer — you can do better than that. You must have got a mindblock last night or something.'

So I sat outside for a day flying some remote-control aeroplanes, had a little drink and came in that evening and nailed it. Sometimes it's the strangest things that give you inspiration!

And that's the thing. If Dappy kicks off a record and it's on an upward vibe, building and building when it comes to my verse, I can't let it start going downhill. I have to build it even further to keep it moving and keep it interesting, otherwise people will get bored of the record.

And we apply that attitude to every word of every part of every song. If even the word 'and'

doesn't sound good in a bar, we'll re-record that whole bit just to get that one word sounding right. We are perfectionists and cannot have anything half-baked because we are too dedicated to be like that.

When it comes to making tracks, me and Dappy structure the whole record. I start the process with the beats for it and throw on a couple of melodies, and then Dappy comes on and we find the best melody then put words to it. Then boom! T will come down to the studio and lay down a hook — she'll write her verse and add her bit to the track.

Before you know it, we've made another smasher!

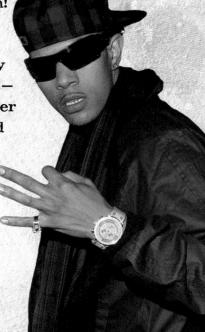

MUSIC, MATES AND A MESSAGE

Even though we're big-selling artists, us lot are just normal day-to-day people. We don't think of ourselves as superstars – we don't really process the fame thing until someone shows us a picture of thousands of fans or something like that. After so long, it just suddenly happened so quickly – the transition from underground success to being A-list artists on shows like *Jonathan Ross* and GMTV.

My family means more to me than ever. These days I don't get too much time to spend with them, so every time I get a chance I want to be with them.

Dappy and Tulisa come first too. They're like family to me. If those two don't approve of something I wanna do in our business, it won't get done. Simple. We're a tripod and if one leg falls, we all fall.

We are a true family. If Dappy's not around, I can still just go and see his mum and chill there for a bit, eat some food and watch some telly. Sometimes I'll go to Tulisa's dad's house and chill with Uncle Stevie even if she's out with her girls. I would have a lonely life if I didn't have them two and other friends that keep my feet planted. Even if it's just to come round to mine and play some Xbox, it means a lot to me.

It's important to keep a real life away from all this madness. I still go through the hood every day and chill with my people there as much as I possibly can – with all the youngsters and the elders. And the thing is, it's those people who see the real me. They don't see me as some big TV star, it's just Fazer innit?

Don't think we don't row sometimes though. Dappy is always getting himself into some sort of stupid shit! Whether it be something to do with the police, or just some argument with Tulisa. Those two are ALWAYS rowing with each other because she's trying to be a grown-up mature woman and Dappy keeps telling her to remember where she came from! She tries to pretend she's a new sophisticated young lady and Dappy says she's just the same as us.

He's always threatening to throw her on the grass like in the old days and tussle with her.

She's not having it though. If me or Dappy start winding her up, she'll pull up her tracksuit bottoms and be like 'Don't start with me, Fazer – I'll knock you out right now.'

Dappy took the piss with me in the studio once. There's always someone who will just conk out first after a long night working and more often than not that person will be me. So I drifted off while Dappy was going through his vocals and he decided to have some fun.

He did some terrible stuff to me – and he filmed it with the same camera we used to make our music videos with. When I saw it later I couldn't believe the stuff he was doing to me. He put his big toe on my lips. Took off his shoe and his sock and pushed his big toe on my lips – moving my lips about and everything. Then he got this marker pen out and started playing noughts and crosses on my face while I was sleeping.

Dappy's mum came in the next morning and woke us up and I could see something was up just from the look in her face and the way she was laughing at me. When I saw my face in the mirror I was screwing. My lips were coloured in black, my finger nails, my eyelids – writing all over my face – he even drew on my glasses.

I went mad. I swore I was going to put hair-removal cream in Dappy's shampoo – and all the time all I could hear was Dappy and his mum cracking up. I'll get him back though!

That's why when we go on tour, Tulisa takes a separate tour bus from us! No one's safe on tour so she plays it sensible. Plus she likes to have her own space, go and have a shower and a sleep in the hotel, do her hair and all that. Us boys are just happy with whatever. We'll sleep wherever we need to, be it the venue, the bus, wherever.

Sometimes touring does get boring, I'm not gonna lie. Performing our old songs can get hard because we just want to show everyone all the new material we have.

I don't really have a pre-show ritual to get myself hyped up. I've been doing it for so long that I'm just kind of ready. The only thing I do really is start jumping up and down on the spot to get my adrenaline going. I think that's left over from the athletics!

When you sit in a studio for so long day and night, working your arse off to try and make the best possible record you can, going on stage is the reward. Seeing 10,000 people singing your vocal back to you without you even saying anything is the most overwhelming feeling that you could ever have.

And you're so much more grateful knowing that you've done it for yourself. If someone was to give me a million pounds tomorrow it would nowhere near amount to that feeling. It's the same whatever your walk of life. If you put the work in, you WILL get the results back and you'll be laughing.

> **We got our skates on to record *Against All Odds* because we wanted to maintain our rise upwards. We did that album in four and a half months. The work rate was crazy. We started at 11 a.m. and worked clean through until 7 a.m., seven days a week for that whole time.**

It's a big album and properly different from our first one. *Uncle B* was made over a period of eight years. It was almost like a 'Best of N-Dubz' because every song on that album had come out before we put the album out. And we still sold 500,000 records. So *Against All Odds* was our chance to show everyone where we are at now. Fresh sounds and our views on the world as we speak. We used it to show fans the stuff that we go through on a daily basis. And the proof is in the pudding. It went platinum in just under a month. That's 300,000 sales. It took us five months to sell that many the first time around.

> The feedback from the fans is special. Our songs are about what they're seeing too and they can relate to our subject matter and to us as young people in the UK today.

Each song has a story and message to it. 'Say It's Over' is a song in there about trying to get out of a relationship because you don't love the person like you used to and how do you do that? Everyone knows that feeling. Then you've got songs like 'Shoulda Put Something On' about teenage pregnancy and promoting safe sex. The song that we wrote with Gary Barlow – 'No One Knows' – is all about the recession that we're all struggling with.

People might have been surprised when we worked with Gary, but we're not closed-minded. It was nice to work with him because he's from a different era and background from us lot, so it was good to see how he worked – plus he learned from us too. It was a steep learning curve for both of us. We all listened to each other and came out writing a great record together.

That song's about us lot trying to fight through it as a team. And when I say team, I mean the community, the country, everyone together. Because I want this place to be a good place to live. That's why I talk about revolution, even if it's just ideas and ways of thinking. I don't want people feeling like there's no chance for them and no opportunities. I want there to be equal opportunities for everyone. All I see is us lot paying taxes for politicians to take the piss with our money. Spending our cash on the Millennium Dome? If they used that money to invest in just one area it would be a different story, but it's wrong the way this country is set up.

In the 10-year journey of N-Dubz I have changed so much to be able to see stuff like that. Nowadays I call myself a spectator of life. I look at life as if I'm on a balcony, looking down at everything, allowing me to analyse situations from an outside perspective. At the same time, I've learned to look at myself and change for the better.

I've calmed down so much. I've become a good-hearted person who actually cares about other people now. At the start of this journey I was angry about everything. I was a rebel without a cause, going against everything with no real reason beyond rage at my situation. But I now know there is always hope – and that's what I want fans to understand.

Not everyone can have a career in music or entertainment like we do, but there's so many other jobs in this business if you want to get involved.

There's no reason why kids from poor background all over the country shouldn't be involved in showbusiness if that's what they want. You just have to have a can-do attitude, not a cannot-do one. That's why we give jobs to people who are from around our way. We'll give someone a wardrobe job to earn them some money on tour. Get them to just get all our clothes ready and that.

They can go further too. One of the guys who manages us came from a place in Nottingham where there's not that much opportunity and he came down to London with nothing. Now he's consulting for major record labels and has his own management company. Anyone can achieve anything if they put their mind to it.

Don't think that being in a business suit and looking smart is geeky. It's all part of playing the game – and it IS all a game. Likewise you shouldn't bow to peer pressure. If you know something's wrong, or it's gonna hold you back, don't let yourself be pushed into doing it. I always tell my little brother Lewis not to follow other people, because if he does his own thing, other people will eventually follow him.

Like me now. I'm getting the opportunity to work with big names – three of the most talented people I've ever worked with in my life being Gary, Mr Hudson and Chipmunk. As a young lyricist, Chipmunk is still developing but his ability is already phenomenal. That's a big star right there.

The problem with Mr Hudson is his inability to finish records! He loves writing so much that he'll start a record then get distracted. When we did 'Playing with Fire' he recorded his first verse and then disappeared into the next room and started playing the piano. I went in after him and he started going on about this new melody he was playing and saying he had a new hit we needed to record right then and there. We hadn't even finished recording the first hit. He's just too talented. I respect him in a big way. Both him and Gary are proper musos.

And now we're ready to step it up even further. 2010 is the year we look to expand beyond these shores. Starting with America and going on from there. We are ready, we have the self-belief and we have the talent.

Even still, we know for a fact out in America it's back to the drawing board – start from scratch time.

Yes, we have done very well here in the UK, but the Americans don't know about us. The kids in America don't speak like us, come from where we come from or live the lifestyle that we live. So now, making new records and going forward, we have to think about how to make ourselves accessible to more than just the British. And not just to the Americans either. We have to make our appeal universal. I have to craft my lyrics so that everyone can understand my messages, be they in the UK, America, Germany or Japan.

Every day is a part of a new journey and we are still developing, still striving and still breaking down new barriers. We still have a lot left to give. The world has only seen 65 per cent of what N-Dubz is capable of achieving. We've got almost as much to give again as we have already. That's why we'll succeed in America.

We're looking to get on as many support slots as we can, do all the promo and interviews and blow up over there too.

> I can't wait to link up with some big American names too. There's one big dream collaboration that I want to put in place. I don't even care if I'm on the record, I'll just make the music. I wanna see Dappy, Akon, R Kelly and Eminem all with their unique voices on a record. That would be sick.
>
> That's just one of the goals I'm still reaching for. I would love to take on issues about politics and the environment and world affairs in the future – no subject is off limits. In ten years' time I would love to have my own label where I can sign and nurture my own artists and keep bringing good music into the world. I want our music to live on through future generations.

The drive still comes from remembering where we started. Sitting around with Uncle B telling us one day you will have tour buses and money in the bank. That day is now, and we are living that dream. We don't take it for granted and we know we have to work every day to deserve it.

DAPPY AND FAZER'S TOP 10 LYRICISTS

It's impossible for us to put these talented artists in order, so you're just gonna have to decide for yourself who is the lyrical don! Keep an open mind and check out all these artists' music. You will hear their influences on us if you listen carefully.

CORMEGA
An old-school master MC

DRAKE
A Canadian rapper — watch for him this year

GEORGE MICHAEL
Guilty feet have got no rhythm. Legend

STYLES P
Proper gangsta

EMINEM
You know who he is

STING
Don't stand so close to me. G'wan Sting!

NAS
Contender for best rapper ever

TUPAC
A poet and commentator

PAPOOSE
Channelling some old-school styles and coming fresh

PHIL COLLINS
One of the best all-round musicians alive

HAPPY TIMES

We tried to be clever when we were writing *Against All Odds* and think about what was current and what people could identify with in our music. But a lot of the influence for the album comes from our own experience too, and the whole point is we are just like everyone else.

> It's not hard to figure out a song like 'Should Have Put Something On' and its message about safe sex comes from Dappy's experiences. He's got a kid and of course he drew on that when he was writing.

If you take any interest in our personal lives, you'll be able to make sense of most of our songs. All in all I really enjoyed recording the *Against All Odds* album. I even got to write my own solo track, and then record the whole thing by myself. I could really express myself musically. It was great.

> The amount of hours we put into making that album, it's not surprising I got a little bit ill. If I'd had a bit more sleep, eaten better and necked some vitamins I would have been in better shape. But at the end of the day it was just flu. It WASN'T swine flu! Thank you very much!

We are still normal people when it really comes down to it. I know in the public's eye I'm seen as a celebrity but I still see all of that as a shallow façade that means nothing. People who are on TV aren't more important than other people. None of us make gold bars when we go to the toilet so whether or not I'm on TV makes no difference.

I know I'm seen as a celebrity – I accept it, I fall into that category, and I do what I have to do and play the game – but I don't feel any different now from how I did before people knew our songs. I still walk out to the shops to get a pint of milk if I need to. I forget how other people see me.

If people do recognise me and start chatting, I'm really laid-back. It's nice having fans and I really appreciate it, so I show them love back. I can remember when I was a kid, if I'd have met Nick Carter I probably would have been the same way, but it's just weird seeing people get like that over me. It's only me! If they saw me waking up in the morning they wouldn't be impressed. Lol. I don't let it go to my head and if people think I'm sexy, well that's nice. I'm half decent and I take it as a compliment.

We have had a hardcore following of fans from very early on. Even when we were just on Channel U, kids would go absolutely mad for us. We'd turn up for a little show and they were just obsessive. They were like little soldiers marching everywhere we would lead them.

I think back then they loved us specifically because we were so unknown. It was like THEIR thing that other people didn't know about. They could go to their parents or their posh cousin and be like 'This is the music I listen to.' It was like a little way of them rebelling.

We loved them from the start. They gave us a reason to be doing it and without them, we wouldn't be where we are right now. We love all our little N-Dublets – that's what we call them.

We get mad fans that turn up to every one of our gigs all over the country. One girl punched a bouncer on stage to get to Dappy. She actually knocked him out – and grabbed a hug off Dappy. Other girls get Dappy and Fazer's names tattooed on their necks. It's mad!

I have some obsessive male fans on MySpace who send me poetry and that kind of thing. There was one scary one. This guy got really specific about what kind of rude stuff he wanted to do with me. He said he used to be obsessed with Mariah Carey but now he loves me! Ha ha ha.

But what I always come back to is my loved ones. I place a lot of importance on friends and family. Now more than ever I need my close friends around me. I love chilling out with my family more than anything. A lot of my family live in Greece and if they come to visit I don't want to miss a second that they're here. I'm proper family oriented. Smelling a kitchen full of food, or chilling with my nan in her room are some of the nicest ways I can think of to spend my time.

But the funny thing is, I'm not broody at all. I couldn't deal with a child now. Hopefully I'll have a kid when I'm 35 or something like that – definitely not younger than 30. I just haven't got that feeling yet. I don't want to spend day and night nurturing someone else. I'm just trying to make myself happy at the moment.

As well as everything is going, I can't say that I'm really happy. Which kind of pisses me off because I feel like I should be. The

depression does still affect me and I do still get little overwhelming feelings of being down, and that needs to go. My ambition is to find out what makes me happy.

And I am getting there. I am happier than I've ever been, and that's a big step for me, but I need to do more soul-searching and stay positive. That can be hard to do sometimes with Dappy and Fazer around! Whenever we fight it's almost always me versus Dappy and Fazer. Or sometimes me and Fazer will be on the same side. But that's rare.

In general we row about the boys' actions. It's very simple. I feel I'm more mature than them and I don't think they always act correctly for this industry. For example, we'll be doing an interview and Dappy will start playing with his necklaces and ignoring the person talking to him.

Afterwards I'll tell him off for coming across rude or arrogant and ask him who he thinks he is. He normally tells me to shut up and says I don't know what I'm talking about. Then it escalates to us screaming at each other and telling each other to rot in hell. Fazer will sometimes get involved and tell Dappy to calm it down.

We might be out at a club and Dappy will start getting all hot under the collar because some guy is looking at him the wrong way. Fazer will pull him aside sometimes and tell him he needs to modify his attitude and stop acting up. Me and Fazer will normally side together to get him to calm down. Dappy doesn't really see any boundaries, and that can be a problem. He lives in Dappy's world.

Our biggest issue and clash point is about the way we conduct ourselves. I like to be very professional whereas the boys don't really give a damn what people think. I see that as bad manners. But I admit, sometimes I'm too hard on them – they're just doing what young lads do, but that's not always acceptable in this scene. It's like they're naughty kids and I'm a stressed mum trying to control them. I'm constantly telling them off, because whatever they do rubs off on me and how people perceive me as well and that's not fair in my eyes.

But that's just our relationship. As people we have different views. They are very good-hearted boys deep down, and I would kill for them. I love them very much, we just don't always get along. Lol.

Life on the road isn't always fun for me because I'm the only chick! We travel separately because we'd actually kill each other if we travelled together. Those two go on the tour bus and I follow in a car and stay in hotels. I hate the tour bus. It makes me claustrophobic and the first time I travelled on it I got motion sickness from being stuck in a smelly box! If by chance they happen to stay in a hotel on a certain night, I make sure they're put on a different floor from me because I need to be away from them or I won't be getting any sleep.

Don't get me wrong, we don't hate each other on the road, it's just we get along better and do better performances if we see each other less. We only really see each other at the venues or perhaps if we all go out. But 90 per cent of the tour is spent actually on the road and so we don't see each other until rehearsal.

When it's time to go on stage I like a little glass of wine or perhaps a JD while I'm getting my hair, make-up and wardrobe ready. When I can hear the crowd chanting from backstage I get that feeling of adrenaline in me. Then I take a few minutes to reflect – I think about how far we've come and then I picture us at the very start in comparison with how we are now. Then I think of Uncle B, say one Hail Mary, one Our Father and then I say, 'Thank you, God, please give me the strength to tear up this show.' And that's it.

The buzz on stage is amazing if I relax and allow myself to enjoy it. Sometimes I do get too caught up in worrying about looking and sounding all right. When I let loose, that's when I enjoy it the most. It's one of the best feelings in the world.

Working with other amazing artists is pretty good too. Chipmunk is someone that I've made a good friend of. I love Chipmunk to pieces. He's one of the most genuine people I've met. He's got a light in him that shows he's one of those people that's good inside. He's someone that I like to be around.

Mr Hudson is hilarious. He's a strange and intriguing character, unlike anyone else I have ever met. I call him The Gentleman, or Sir Ben III, because he's got such a posh voice and such good manners. He'll kiss my hand and make sure I'm okay when we're in the studio – proper old-fashioned.

Gary Barlow is such a chilled-out guy – probably too chilled in fact. To the extent that we'll just end up falling asleep when we're

supposed to be writing a song together. Lol. He's got this laid-back kind of vibe where he doesn't get excited about much, but he is sooooo talented. We sit down, crack open a few beers and have a curry. He doesn't behave like a big superstar at all.

Even with all this success, there's no way that I think we've got as high as we're gonna get. We're gonna up the ante now, that's it! With this new album done, now I'm a little bit scared! With *Against All Odds* doing so well, we have to step up another level and go global. We need to reach the millions and break America. Find that next level and break down that door. I mean, we could always live off going platinum with every album we release in the UK once a year. But that's not good enough. Now we want to get to the level of Beyonce and all those really big acts and take over the world. Mwahahaaa!

> **In ten years' time I want to be right at the top. Simple as. That's why we're going to America. It's scary as it means starting from scratch all over again. It's a whole new market and I'm scared but excited. This is the new thing for me now. I've set myself a new goal and I'm going to work at it – because I like a challenge to keep me mentally stimulated.**

I have no idea what's in store for me other than a hell of a lot of hard work and maybe even empty shows again. But I'm happy to do it all over again. If nothing else, I will learn from it and learning is always a good thing.

> You only live once and the main thing in life is to be positive, do the best you can and try to be happy. No matter where you are or what you doing, there's no point in anything unless you are happy.

BACKSTAGE RIDER

Red Bull – although we're trying
to give the energy drinks a miss now

A bottle of chilled white wine
and some glasses

Capri Sun drinks because they're
nicer than water but still good for you

Bottle of Jack Daniels.
We have a shot before stage and a shot
to have on stage to keep us bubbly

Nando's chicken – lemon and
herb of course with perinaise sauce

Twiglets, McCoys crisps and
a selection of chocolate bars

A mixture of other foods,
fish and chips and some salads

Towels and a barber to make
sure the boys' hair is trimmed

A stereo to link the N-Dubz iPod
to and get in the mood

A full-length mirror
for Dappy and Fazer and a
room full of mirrors for Tulisa!

A proper comfy couch
in case Fazer needs to conk out

ALL YOU NEED IS LOVE

When it came to making *Against All Odds* we knew we just had to lock down in the studio. I had so many big tunes in my head that I had to get them down. We worked solidly for about four months with no ease-ups, just cracking out tunes. Even still, I'd be happy to release any song off there as a single. If there's a better or more relevant album in the UK from 2009 then I need to hear about it.

We're on top of the world now, and the fans are the people who have kept us on track. Any time someone tries to throw a little spanner in the works, I think about the fans and I immediately know what they would want us to do.

I've got so much love for them. Every now and then I go on our own official N-Dubz page to see who the biggest fans are and give them some personal love back. I am the best guy to the fans, believe me.

Sometimes after a performance, I come off stage and feel like I'm floating and that my work is done, everyone loves us and that's it. Bun dat! Soon enough I remember I need to carry on going and wow the next 5,000 fans and the next – it's always a pleasure.

That's not to say some things aren't still difficult. I am happier now than I was when times were hard, but there's a lot of different stresses that I never used to have in my life. For example, nowadays I can't just walk out of my house and walk down the street anywhere really. I still can around where I grew up, or if I'm with my boys, but by myself I just can't do it any more in case I get mobbed.

Some people will try and hug me or kiss me, someone else might try and punch me in my head when I'm not looking, someone else might try and stab me and rob my chains. It's hard to stay out of trouble when trouble is looking for you. That's why I've had a few cases over the last year where someone's tried to take my chain or start shit because of who I am. And now I've got my boy to look out for too so I have to make double sure I stay out of trouble.

I love my little Gino – even if he does get sick on me! He's really brought out my softer side and I feel a bit nicer now. When I'm around him I'm aware that I have responsibilities to someone else now. I am still learning and I have to remember that when I'm looking after him and his mum Kaye isn't about, I can't just walk off into the other room and leave him. I'm slowly learning that I have to do all the boring stuff as well. This is a new stage in life for me and I'm starting from scratch.

This is the point where my dad would have come into play again. He would have taught me how to be a dad myself, showed me where I was going wrong and given me some pointers. I'm having to find out on my own with no guidance. I still have to be told to feed him, I won't realise he needs to eat. As soon as I'm told, of course I will do it, but it's a steep learning curve for me.

Any time I was being rude when I was younger, I'd get black pepper in my mouth or a little slap to make sure I knew I was out of order.

When Gino's big enough he will get discipline from me most definitely. He's going to be brought up with proper manners and he's going to be able to grow up with the life that I wasn't able to have.

Already he's got so much more than I had growing up. But me and Kaye are going to make sure he knows where his mum and dad came from. Just because he's living nice, it doesn't mean he won't know it's not like this for everyone.

He's going to go to a normal junior school in Camden, or Hammersmith, or wherever is local to where we live. That's where he'll learn how to deal with people and interact, and then afterwards he's going to a stage school like Sylvia Young or something. That's where he can get his grades and he can nurture any talent he has creatively.

I would not recommend anyone have children until they are totally ready to. Both financially and emotionally. I'm lucky that I now have the money for a good life so I can bring my son up with a good life.

Bringing a child into the world is no small thing – it's another life and you HAVE to take that responsibility very seriously indeed.

Being a family man keeps me grounded. I'll do a show in front of thousands of people screaming out my name like I'm their idol, then come home and get called a wanker by Kaye! She'll just put me in my place.

And I need that even though life on the road is the best. That's the good stuff. The travelling is amazing. You're on the tour bus having jokes, living from hotel to hotel and you never know what the next city is going to have for you.

I don't need to get hyped up before a show because I'm just hyper anyway. My life is going on beforehand, be it arguments, money matters, personal matters – that's all that's running through my head until the last minute before I step on stage.

I know what I'm all about on stage and it's like a switch. The minute I put my show clothes on and my Dappy hat on, that's it. I'm the showman. I limber up, do my little stretches from karate and then bound on stage because I know what the fans want. As soon as I see them, I know what to give them. Just a few words from one of our great songs and they're singing straight back at me. That's it. We've won them. There's no nerves for me.

The tour bus is a hectic place, and me and Fazer will bring a couple of friends on there with us. We've got a couple of laptops on there because when you're on tour you want to be interacting with the fans more than ever.

I'll go on late at night and start taking pictures of us lot for the fans to see what we're getting up to.

I know I pissed people off on the Christmas 2009 tour because I kept stealing everyone's phone so I could call Kaye and my baby. My phone was missing at the time so I'd wait for someone to fall asleep then use up all the credit on their phone calling her.

People's always trying to play pranks on each other on the bus but no one ever gets me because I'm too quick. If you fall asleep on there when people's still awake, boy, you've got it coming to you. One time Fazer woke me up from my bunk to show me what they

had done to this girl who was on the tour with us. I couldn't believe it when I saw her. It was worth waking up for. They had put strips of kebab all over her face, some salad on her eyes and some chips in her nose. She looked like Predator, I swear!

That's why you won't see T on our tour bus. She knows that can happen to her too if she was to roll with us. She travels separately with our tour manager and does her girl stuff in the hotel.

What would really drive me mad would be how T will stall ANYTHING by taking so much time to get ready. Even if it's just us three in the studio I'll tell her to be there for two and she's not there because she's doing her hair or something pointless. She knows she has to do something and she'll make up the dumbest excuse for why she's gonna be late. And whatever I say she'll just keep talking until I run out of things to say to her. She knows she's wrong, but she won't accept it!

Talking about wrong things – don't even get me started on *The X Factor*. Our record 'I Need You' went to No. 5. At No. 1 was Black Eyed Peas, 2 was Leona Lewis, 3 JLS, 4 Cheryl Cole. All of them were on *X Factor* in the weeks before. You take them out of the equation and boom! N-Dubz are No. 1 and miles ahead of anyone else for weeks. That gets to me.

I respect *The X Factor* for people like Leona and JLS. And I do like them lot on a personal level. But – JLS had to stand in a queue with a thousand other people waiting to go into an audition and no one gave a damn about them. Four boys standing in a line, so

what? The morning after they did that audition and it went on telly – they were famous. They stood in one queue and the very next day people are screaming at them, trying to get a picture with them and whatever. Even if they never made it through the audition they'd still have had a little fan base to build on. By the time they're up near the final, they've got so many people following them. Sometimes I think that ain't fair. I worked for 10 years and all they did was go on *X Factor*!

When you go to a show now, JLS and N-Dubz are the main names. Those are the two names you see everyone go crazy for. We're on the same level now despite all that work we had to put in. Maybe they're a little bigger than us – but that's the power of the X.

I would love to go on *X Factor* just to piss Simon Cowell off. I met Simon out in Barbados. I went up to him and said 'What you sayin', big man?'

And he said, 'Hello Dappy. Congratulations on your success. It's not in my type of area, but you three are great. It's all about selling records which is what you guys are doing, so make sure you carry on pushing.'

But I know he's pissed off. I know he looks in the charts, sees we sold more than Alexandra Burke's album with *Against All Odds* and is screwing about it! There's no way he's inviting us on his show so we can start knocking his artists off the top of the charts.

I want to prove to him that you don't have to go on *The X Factor* to sell records. But at the same time, if he DOES ask us on, we'll go on that show and make that show something special. We'd go on

there and do a great, live vocal performance. What I'm saying is we are big without Mr Cowell's help – it can be done!

Certain artists – I don't wanna name names – release their records when no other big names are coming out. That means you can go to No. 1 with 32,000 sales. N-Dubz went to No. 5 with almost twice as many sales as that. When people get excited about their album going to No. 2 or something with 70,000 sales and we're there with half a million sales and not even making the Top 5, it bugs me. It doesn't represent the truth. *Against All Odds* sold more than Kanye West and Kaiser Chiefs!

Even still, when I heard the guy out of Take That liked us, my eyebrows were raised up. Gary Barlow is a great lad. He approached us to get involved because he was feeling what we were doing. We respect him for taking time out of his heavy schedule to come and write with underdogs like us. He's a down-to-earth character and did all the normal stuff you do. He took a picture with Gino, stayed with us for two days of writing and he LOVES his curry. We ate so much curry. But most of all that man knows how to write a song, so we learned a lot from him. It's a possibility that the song we did with Gary – 'No One Knows' – might even be our next single. If we don't run out of steam – that's a joke by the way!

I was feeling tired after 10 years of grafting – but now I've found Barbados. That's my new place I'm telling you. I wanna go there twice a month! I know some people there now and I wanna make that place my home from home. I came back from jet-skiing there and I'm all refreshed and ready for another 10 years of hard work. The day I finish the Against All Odds tour, I'm straight off to Barbados with Kaye and Gino and a couple of other people.

Then America is the next big plan. We'll go there and start straight off with the grafting if that's want they want. We'll fly there for one meeting, or we'll fly there for eight weeks of work, because N-Dubz is going on to even bigger tings and that can only come from work.

You get no world domination without putting in elbow grease, that's one thing I've learned. I'd be more than happy to spend three months over there and record another album for worldwide release. We'd fling in maybe six of our big songs from our first two albums, then write six or seven more smashers to put on there and make it a big dynamite ting to hit everyone with, bam!

That's the goal now. Keep every one of our loyal UK fans happy, but go on and spread the N-Dubz word to the rest of the world. And we'll be able to avoid any of the mistakes we made getting here when we go to America. We'd be looking to hook up with proper big artists over there for a collaboration so we can arrive with a bang.

Akon and Drake are two artists who immediately spring to mind that I would love to work with. Me and Tulisa would sort out a massive hook and Fazer would do the beat and boom! We'd bring the melody to them. N-Dubz is here to make a big chorus for you and we'll let rappers come in and sit on the beat and do their job. Our sound will modify even more but still keep that essence of N-Dubz that the fans love.

We're gonna be Black Eyed Peas level and reach No. 1 in 15 countries with platinum album sales all over the world. That will happen. I can say that because back in the day we said we were going to be No. 1 and get famous and everyone told us we were wrong. And here we are.

"I KNOW. N-DUBZ 2010, BIG TINGS. NANANIIIIII."

ACKNOWLEDGEMENTS

DAPPY

If I forget anyone I'm sorry.

I want to especially thank my mum and dad for raising me right!!!

I wanna thank Kaye, my son Gino, my brother Spi, all of my family in Greece, Toula, Yaya Koula, R.I.P. Grandad Costas. Thanks to Grandad Spi, I love you. Plantanos (my home little village), Lickourgos cafe!

I wanna thank my hood for making me who I am today!

I want to thank C, Lulu, my younger Fefe, all my youngers from Shipton Blocks! Free Bobby! Duku yourself Yoggs, Ztvdee, Kat Park, Benit Court, Ross, Basco Camden, Rocco!!! Love you all!

Special thanks to Richard Castillo.

Big thanks to Jonathan Shalit for pulling all the strings and getting us the big slots and making it all happen, very professional – and thanks for your red socks as well!

Big up my management assistant Dean.

I wanna big up Naz, Matt, CriS, Brian and everyone at AATW/Universal, Rak at Sony ATV and Dennis Ingoldsby.

I want to big up Simon Jones, John Keane, Charlie Lycett, Joggs, Lucy, Kat, Stacy Cherry Lips, Maurice and all my promo team.

Big thanks to Mark and Naylor.

Thanks to everyone at HarperCollins for believing in us and letting us put our story down in words especially Vicky McGeown, Natalie Jerome, Jess Carey and Laura Summers.

Big thanks to Joe Mott – you put our words down in our own voices when others wouldn't have.

A special thanks to the whole of Radio 1 for always supporting us. Thanks to Paola at Adidas.

Thanks to Kelvin our mix engineer, Harry and Ross at Fisher Lane.

I want to say a huge thanks to Tulisa and Fazer.

I also want to thank Gary Barlow, Wiley, Chipmunk, Tinchy and Nivo for appearing on the album.

R.I.P. Uncle B – if it weren't for you, like I told you, you are the best.

Love you all!

TULISA

First of all, I'd like to thank Uncle B, the man with a plan – we wouldn't be here without you. I know you're looking down on us and I know you're proud, I miss you and I love you with all my heart. I'd like to thank God for blessing me with a voice and the opportunity to use it, for giving me strength in times of weakness and listening to my prayers. Please continue to show me light and help me to become a better person and all that I can be.

Thanks to the fans – I love you for life! Thanks to my mum and dad for supporting my dreams and making me the person I am today, love you.

Thanks to all my family for their love and support, Spi, Maz, Georgy, Adam, Yaya, Pappous, Aunty Zoe, Aunty Moira, Aunty Paula, Uncle Apollo, Aunty Lu, Trevor, Oliver, Kay, Gino, Havana, Niamh, Vags, Vasia, Grandad Tom, Hollis, Oisin, Phelim, Uncle Mick, Aunty Linda, Goldman, Uncle John, Grace, Aunty Jill, Aunty Shaz.

I love you all very much.

Thanks to my record label AATW/Universal, Matt, Cris, Naz and Brian.

Thanks to HarperCollins for having faith in us – hopefully this is the start of many books with you.

Joe Mott – you are a good guy. Thank you.

Thank you to George Burt, Ben, MG, Danno, ROAR Global; Rich Castillo, Jonathan Shalit, Dean, Nick Canham and Dolapo.

Simon Jones, Charlie Lycett, Jenny, Jason, Scotty, Claire, Chris Panayi, Steven Luckman, Mark Sutton, Paola, Naylor, Gary Howard, Michelle – love you girl! John Grey, Timz, Breakbeat, Harry and everyone at Fisher Lane, Chairworks Studios, Kelvin, Tom, James, Kash, Audi, Ross, Radio One, special big up to Max, Kiss 100, Gordan, MOBOs, Kanya King, *Dubplate Drama*, Luke, Rankin, Darren Platt, Bliss for giving me my first front cover, Amber. Thank you to all my friends Ny Ny, Mercedes, Kat, Coco, Soly, Miranda, Angela, Abuk, Nova Caine, Michelle, Ricci.

Special thanks to Justin for simply makin me happy, ha ha love you puffin … I'm your thumper for life! LOL xxx.

Loads of love to my little princess Tyla, big up Kyley boy MC LOL and lots of love to Marie. HA HA. Shouts out to Chrissy and Ripper, Platinum, Michelle, Aron, Kelly La Rock, Chipmunk, Mr Hudson, Wiley, Tinchy, Ironik, Mz Bratt and last but not least thanks to my little brothers Dappy and Faze for making my life as stressful as possible … kidding … not! LOVE YA! And big up to Fefe, Zee, C & Lewis! Peace!

FAZER

First, I would like dedicate an extra special thank you to the fans – life wouldn't be what it is right now without you guys, so send a shout out to yourselves DUKU!!!

I want to thank my Mumzy, Pups and my two brothers for their love and support over the last 10 years!!

I want to thank all my goons, my n***a 'C', Zee TvD my DAWG, Dee-Bo, Yogz, Basco, 3 Bobby Cha LB4 Dun Know!! Fefe, Dappy and Tulisa for all staying real, loyal and keeping man level headed!! BLESS!!

I wanna thank my other half for standing by me all this time – u kept me from drowning at one point and kept my head above the water! And I love you for that!! Thank you Babe!! x

I wanna thank Jonathan Shalit and everyone at ROAR Global who helped sail the ship in the right direction: Rich Castillo, Dean Coulson, Severine Berman, Nick Canham, Jenny Vine, Lea Evans, Dolapo Alafe-Aluko and Tina Andrews.

Thanks to all the guys that have made this book happen: Natalie, Vicky, Jess, Laura and Joe. There'll be more to come – I know it.

Thank you to Kelvin (Afreex) for mixing the album and the *Uncle B* album!! Sounds tight bruv!!

Big shout out to Ross and Amir for taking the world off mine and Dappy's back for the vocal engineering on the album.

Thank you to everyone at Fisher Lane studios! Geoff, Harry, Dale and Carol!! Nice one guys! James and Tom Fuller at Chairworks! Thanks.

Thank you to everyone at AATW, Matt and Cris, thanks for having the faith! Naz Idelji and Brian Berg at U Music for getting things done, everyone at Lucid PR John Keane, Joggs Canfield, Lucy Honey and the rest of the people in the office. Simon Jones at Hackford Jones PR, Chris Panayi our accountant, Gary Howard and everyone at Marshall Arts, Stacey at Cherry Lips, our tour managers and security Mark Sutton and Naylor Harrington!! Our production manager John Gray, Timz for all them long hours pulling stuff together! Breakbeat for bad boy drumz on da stage and in da stoodz!!! Michelle Duverney our choreographer, Jenny Kirby and Jason Brookes our hair and make up team! Scotty and Bianca our stylists!! Big Up!!!!

And last but never ever forgotten – UNCLE B!!

The motivation behind the graft and the reason we all so dedicated to what we do!!

This one's for you!!!!!

Love!!!

HarperCollins*Publishers*
77–85 Fulham Palace Road,
Hammersmith, London W6 8JB

www.harpercollins.co.uk

First published by HarperCollins*Publishers* 2010

10 9 8 7 6 5 4 3 2 1

A catalogue record of this book is available from
the British Library

ISBN 978-0-00-736386-5

Printed and bound in Great Britain by Butler Tanner
& Dennis Ltd, Frome, Somerset

Mixed Sources
Product group from well-managed
forests and other controlled sources
www.fsc.org   Cert no. SW-COC-001806
© 1996 Forest Stewardship Council

FSC is a non-profit international organisation established to
promote the responsible management of the world's forests.
Products carrying the FSC label are independently certified
to assure consumers that they come from forests that are
managed to meet the social, economic and ecological needs
of present and future generations.

Find out more about HarperCollins and the environment at
www.harpercollins.co.uk/green

PICTURE CREDITS

Photographs © Ian McManus with the exception of: p. 2, 5, 34,
37, 46, 106, 165 © Steve Goudie; p. 7, 131, 146 © Andrew
Box Photography; p. 55, 59, 93, 111, 121, 156, 178 © Ralph
Petts; p. 5, 40, 45, 83, 139, 152-3, 176, 186 © Philip Rawson;
p. 20, 28, 33, 53, 119 © Tula Contostavlos; p. 33, 36, 124, 181
© Dino Contostavlos; p. 12, 17, 19 © Richard Rawson;
p. 168 © www.thebreakthrough.co.uk

Photographs from fans: p. 2, 4, 60, 69

AGAINST ALL ODDS TOUR 2010

**WE WANT TO THANK THESE GUYS
FOR ALL THEIR HELP ON THE TOUR**

Jonathan Shalit .... Management

Rich Castillo. .... Management

Dean Ondrus-Coulson .. Management

Gary Howard .... Booking agent

SJM .... Promoters

John Gray...... Production Manager

Laura McInnes . Production Assistant

Michelle Duvernay. . . Choreographer

Chris 'Bronski' Jablonski ....
.... Sound Engineer (Monitors)

Dave Lamb ... Sound Engineer (FOH)

Peter Watts....... Lighting Designer

Lewis Young .... Backline Tech

Martin Anderson .... Guitarist

Aaron Fagen .... Drummer

Mark Sutton .... Tour manager

Naylor Charrington .... Security

Kerry Donald. .... Wardrobe

Danny Oakes ....
...... Firebrand Live Merchandising

Roxy Hayde ....
...... Firebrand Live Merchandising

**AGAINST ALL ODDS THE
PLATINUM SELLING ALBUM
IS AVAILABLE TO BUY NOW.**

TO CHART LIFE